101 RECIPES FOR MAKING WILD WINES AT HOME:

A Step-by-Step Guide to Using Herbs, Fruits, and Flowers

By John N. Peragine Jr.

101 RECIPES FOR MAKING WILD WINES AT HOME: A STEP-BY-STEP GUIDE TO USING HERBS, FRUITS, AND FLOWERS

Library of Congress Cataloging-in-Publication Data

Peragine, John N., 1970-
  101 recipes for wild wines at home : a step-by-step guide to using herbs, fruits, and flowers / John N. Peragine, Jr.
    p. cm.
  Includes bibliographical references and index.
  ISBN-13: 978-1-60138-359-4 (alk. paper)
  ISBN-10: 1-60138-359-2 (alk. paper)
  1. Wine and wine making--Amateurs' manuals. I. Title. II. Title: One hundred one recipes for wild wines at home.
  TP548.2.P47 2009
  641.8'72--dc22
                        2009030830

Printed in the United States

PROJECT MANAGER: Kim Fulscher • kfulslcher@atlantic-pub.com
PEER EDITOR: Marilee Griffin • mgriffin@atlantic-pub.com
INTERIOR DESIGN: Samantha Martin • smartin@atlantic-pub.com
ASSISTANT EDITOR: Amy Moczynski • amoczynski@atlantic-pub.com

Printed on Recycled Paper

We recently lost our beloved pet "Bear," who was not only our best and dearest friend but also the "Vice President of Sunshine" here at Atlantic Publishing. He did not receive a salary but worked tirelessly 24 hours a day to please his parents. Bear was a rescue dog that turned around and showered myself, my wife, Sherri, his grandparents Jean, Bob, and Nancy, and every person and animal he met (maybe not rabbits) with friendship and love. He made a lot of people smile every day.

We wanted you to know that a portion of the profits of this book will be donated to The Humane Society of the United States. *–Douglas & Sherri Brown*

The human-animal bond is as old as human history. We cherish our animal companions for their unconditional affection and acceptance. We feel a thrill when we glimpse wild creatures in their natural habitat or in our own backyard.

Unfortunately, the human-animal bond has at times been weakened. Humans have exploited some animal species to the point of extinction.

The Humane Society of the United States makes a difference in the lives of animals here at home and worldwide. The HSUS is dedicated to creating a world where our relationship with animals is guided by compassion. We seek a truly humane society in which animals are respected for their intrinsic value, and where the human-animal bond is strong.

Want to help animals? We have plenty of suggestions. Adopt a pet from a local shelter, join The Humane Society and be a part of our work to help companion animals and wildlife. You will be funding our educational, legislative, investigative and outreach projects in the U.S. and across the globe.

Or perhaps you'd like to make a memorial donation in honor of a pet, friend or relative? You can through our Kindred Spirits program. And if you'd like to contribute in a more structured way, our Planned Giving Office has suggestions about estate planning, annuities, and even gifts of stock that avoid capital gains taxes.

Maybe you have land that you would like to preserve as a lasting habitat for wildlife. Our Wildlife Land Trust can help you. Perhaps the land you want to share is a backyard— that's enough. Our Urban Wildlife Sanctuary Program will show you how to create a habitat for your wild neighbors.

So you see, it's easy to help animals. And The HSUS is here to help.

2100 L Street NW • Washington, DC 20037 • 202-452-1100
www.hsus.org

Dedication

"I dedicate this book to the youngest vintages in our family: my great niece Sailor Addison McCall and my niece Ellamina Rose Held."

Table of Contents

Foreword

John Peragine encapsulates the essence of basic winemaking in his book *101 Recipes for Making Wild Wines at Home: A Step-by-Step Guide to Using Herbs, Fruits, and Flowers.* His simplified style of writing and the contributions of actual input from amateur winemakers creatively bring an age-old art craft into your everyday life. At an average cost of $2/bottle, making your own wine can be achieved without a huge investment.

From the beginning, the book captures the reader's intrigue. Peragine winds you steadily through the organic processes and chemistry, holds a walk-through of the basic equipment needs and functions, then leads into an amazingly unique collection of some of the most fabulous wine recipes I've ever seen. They are made from anything and everything that grows — wild or cultivated. Throughout the book, Peragine scatters anecdotal bits of humor and case studies to light the way to the readers' imaginations. The mountain of information is logically organized and explained with pictures in a very practical manner. It contains more than enough to get you started if you are simply curious and plenty to take you to the next level if you are completely serious. Naturally, as with any detailed process, there are many variations to the winemaking methods described in the book. But through hands-on experimentation and preferences, all winemakers eventually develop their own unique form of the age-old art, and you will too. Over time, a winemaker figures out what they personally like to drink and what has the best results for their own purposes.

Making wine typically starts as a hobby that offers an endless learning experience for anyone who is challenged to improve the next vintage. Each recipe requires three basic ingredients: sugar, acid, and yeast mixed in the right proportions with water. Then the fun begins, with adding wild ingredients. Anyone can make a wine that is quite drinkable for very little cost. At $2/bottle, you have little to lose. Taken seriously or for fun, the hobby of winemaking can develop into a sophisticated business or simply a unique way of creating pleasure and sharing it with friends and family through the ritual celebration of life. From the first batch, you will be hooked!

Cheers to a happy life with wine,

Lynn Keay

Introduction to Winemaking

One Sunday morning, I received a phone call from a friend who asked me to come over for breakfast. At the time I was a poor college student, so the idea of a free home cooked meal was too good to pass up. When I arrived a formidable stack of pancakes and a wine glass full of a yellow sparkling liquid greeted me.

I asked my friend what the drink was and he said it was his newest batch of mead. I had never heard of mead, but he assured me that I would not go blind drinking it. I checked my watch and determined it had to be 5 o'clock somewhere and tried it. It was sweet with a hint of citrus. I was immediately struck by how drinkable and delicious it was.

As I inhaled my pancakes and filled my glass from the green unlabelled bottle, I asked him how he made it. Once he described to me the simple process, I was hooked. I began creating wine right away using nothing more than a bucket, yeast, and a couple of cans of frozen Welch's® Grape Juice Concentrate. I cannot say that it was the best-tasting stuff in the world, but the fact that I was able to transform grape juice into wine created an obsession within me.

I bought basic winemaking equipment and a wine book, and got to work. That was 18 years ago, and my house and garage are full of wine, empty wine bottles, and equipment. My wife has been tolerant because she loves the new wines I create for her to try. Every Christmas, I always have the perfect gifts to give to family and friends.

I warn you, once you start making your own wine, you will not be able to stop. The basic process is simple, but the subtle variations in ingredients, maturation time, and other variables are what make the process so intriguing. Every batch of wine you create will take on a character and life of its own. You may even want to enter your wines in some amateur winemaking competitions. I have found these to be both exciting and a good way to get feedback about how to improve on your wines. In the appendix you will find a list of different competitions around the United States.

In these times of economic uncertainty, it is nice to know that you will be able to create wonderful wine for about $2 a bottle. The price can vary depending on the ingredients, but to make your own wine is not an overly expensive hobby. Once you buy some basic equipment, all you will have to buy are the ingredients. All of the recipes I have included will create either one gallon or five gallons of wine, though each of the one-gallon recipes can be adapted to create five gallons. Five gallons of wine will make approximately 25 average-sized 750ml wine bottles.

Making wine is a social hobby. It is one that you can include friends and family in during the process. I still call my pancake-making friend over to make wine, even after 18 years. I have been a part of different winemaking clubs around the area I live in. Being a member of such a group helps to cut down on the cost of making larger batches of wine and helps defray the cost of purchasing larger, more expensive equipment. In a later chapter I will give you tips on how to create a winemaking club of your own.

This book is about wild wines. These are wines that go beyond using just grapes as the base, but it is also important that you learn the basic winemaking process of making red and white grape wine. The majority of the recipes you will find in this book use different ingredients, such as berries, apples, honey, and even vegetables.

Is Winemaking Legal?

"By making this wine vine known to the public, I have rendered my country as great a service as if I had enabled it to pay back the national debt."
Thomas Jefferson

Until 1979 it was not legal to produce wine at home without a permit. The federal government waived that requirement, but there are still a few restrictions. You can produce 100 gallons of wine per year for a single person or 200 gallons per year per household. You cannot sell nor distill your wine. The winemaking described in this book is for amateur hobbyists. If you wish to produce more than 200 gallons a year then you should apply for the permits needed to open up your own winery business.

How much is 200 gallons of wine? If 5 gallons of wine produces 25 bottles, then 200 gallons would produce 1,000 bottles of wine. You would have to drink almost three bottles of wine a day for a year to consume that much wine. Most people do not come near that amount. I generally try to create a five-gallon batch every month or two. Even at that rate, I am producing 300 bottles of wine a year. This is one of the reasons I have included so many one-gallon recipes. It gives you the chance to produce more varieties of wine without having to move out of your home or digging a large wine cellar. Besides, producing 100 gallons of wine can begin to be cost prohibitive. It is much easier to dump one gallon of wine than it is to dump five gallons of wine. You will not have as much invested in one gallon of ingredients than you would five gallons. Make sure you read the section near the end of this book called "Tales from the Vineyard." You will learn that many experienced winemakers have a story about a failed batch of wine. Every home winemaker I ever met has more than one story of a failed batch. It comes with the territory.

A Brief History of Winemaking

The process of creating wine is a relatively simple one. In fact, spontaneous fermentation of fruit juice happens all the time without human intervention. There are many different stories about how winemaking first began, but none are confirmable. The generally accepted idea is that juice or some other fermentable sugar, such as honey, found its way into water. This could have occurred after a rainstorm in which the honey and water mixture sat. Wild yeasts took over and created a natural brew.

What I wonder is who was the brave soul who first tried a natural wine? What did it taste like? Was it the result of a dare? Someone used their hands to scoop up the brew, drank it, and probably experienced the world's first hangover. For whatever reason, someone actually tried it a second time and winemaking has been an integral part of man's culture and history ever since.

Winemaking is quite ancient and reaches back to Neolithic times. It was during the period when man was settling down and beginning to domesticate plants and animals. It is thought that serious winemaking started when clay vessels were made for the purpose of wine storage.

In 1968, Mary M. Voigt excavated a site in the Zagros Mountains of Iran, where she discovered a yellow residue in the bottom of a jar. The jar was big enough to hold about 9 liters (2.5 gallons) and was located with five other jars in the area of a structure that was thought to be a kitchen. In 1996, when technology became available to analyze such residues, it was confirmed the residue was in fact wine. This ancient wine was named Chateau Hajji Firuz and dated circa 5,400 to 5,000 B.C.E.

It is believed ancient winemaking expanded from Iran and was shipped to places on the Euphrates and Tigris rivers. Later the trade routes from this area were cut off and winemaking practices grew in urban areas.

Domesticated grape plants were transplanted in the mid-3rd century B.C.E throughout Europe, Asia, and Africa. There are Assyrian reliefs that showed men and women lounging under grape arbors drinking what could be inferred to be wine.

Since these ancient beginnings, winemaking has continued to be a regular practice around the world and touches about every continent and culture. You will learn these ancient techniques and create wines your family and friends will love. The problem will be making enough to keep up with the demand.

In the next chapter you will learn the basics of making wine at home. You will be amazed at how simple it is and you may wonder why you had not done so sooner. My family is from Italy and Ireland. There was never a shortage of wine on the dinner table or part of holiday celebrations. My family used to produce their own wine for the family to consume, but we knew some families produced enough wine for extended families or even their communities to share. I now hand down this tradition to you to enjoy with your family and friends.

Sit, relax, and enjoy a homebrewed glass of wine.

CHAPTER 1

Winemaking Basics

Winemaking is so basic that convicts even try to do it in prison toilets, but I would strongly urge you not to attempt this type of wild wine. The results might be wild, just not the kind of wild you would want to consume.

What makes winemaking so simple is that you only need three things to accomplish it, and all of them can be found in nature. In the introduction, I mentioned the first wines were believed to have just "happened." The three elements occurred together and wine spontaneously formed.

The three basic elements that all wine contains are water, some sort of sugar, and yeast. The process goes something like this:

Warning: the next explanation could make you put down your glass of wine and never drink a drop again. The reality is not for the faint of heart.

Water is the essential building block of life. As you will learn, the pretty, ruby-colored wine you love to drink is actually alive. Water is essential because yeast needs it in order to thrive. Water is also the universal solvent, and so it provides a medium for the yeast to have access to the sugar that is dissolved within the liquid.

Yeast loves sugar, and uses it for most of its biological functions; it eats, grows, procreates, and dies. It is through the biological process of living yeast that transforms sugar into alcohol. There are some lengthy biology and chemistry reactions that occur, but knowing just the basic process is sufficient in creating world-class wine.

Yeast consumes sugar because it is essential to its metabolic processes. Yeast metabolism is not that different from the human digestion process. When we digest food, we also transform it into a different form, whether it is gas, liquid, or solid. Energy is drawn from the sugar we eat and what the body does not need is excreted. In the case of yeast, it is alcohol and gas. The gas is in the form of little tiny bubbles. It is those same bubbles you find in champagne and is composed of carbon dioxide, which is the same gas that humans expel when we breathe.

Once the wine reaches a certain level of alcohol, the yeast will die and the process of fermentation will cease. In some cases not all the yeast dies, but is instead in a state of suspended animation. You have seen this state if you have ever opened a packet of yeast to make bread. It is dried and visually lifeless until water is added to it. Wine yeast comes in the same kind of packets bread yeast does.

Never use bread yeast to make wine. You will regret the decision and will quickly pour it down the drain. Bread yeast will leave a bad aftertaste in your wine. It is great at leavening bread but it is not so great at creating alcohol.

If the temperature of the wine rises or sugar is added, this yeast can come back to life. For a home winemaker, this is akin to making liquid hand grenades. The corks and bottles will literally explode, and will redecorate part of your house all the way to the ceiling.

I will give you tips throughout this book on how to avoid this, although if you make wine for long enough, this will probably happen at least once. Just be prepared and do not place your bottled wine next to any nice furniture.

I created raspberry mead once and placed the bottles in my dining room. While I was watching television about a week later, there was a popping sound. It was not loud, but it sounded like popcorn beginning to pop in a microwave. I went to investigate and there was pink liquid dripping from the ceiling. That was quite a mess to clean up. As you will learn later in the book, you must make sure the wine has stopped fermenting before you bottle it.

If you combine the three essential ingredients, you can create just about any kind of wine. The sugars in wine are sucrose and glucose. You cannot use artificial sweeteners to create wine, which is why you will never find sugar-free or diet wine. It is sugar combined with alcohol that gives you the perception of sweetness in wine. In dry wines, the yeast consumes most of the sugar before fermentation ends, and in sweet wines the yeast will die off before consuming all the available sugar.

The natural acids found in fruit, or acid additives that are added to the wine, create the acidic taste in wine. One of the most common acids used in wine is citric acid.

Phenols, which are chemicals found in fruit and grapes, create the bitter taste in wine; they are are usually in the form of tannins. Tannins give red wine its ruby color and astringent taste. There are more phenols found in red wines. Currently there are a number of research studies being conducted about the health benefits of wine tannins.

> There are more than 1,000 different chemicals that can be found in wine; it is made up of 95 percent water and alcohol. The other 5 percent of chemicals give wine its many different possible flavor variations.

In this book, you will learn to create wines using different forms of sugar. Most plants contain some amount of sugar, as it is needed for growth and energy. Fruits contain more sugars than other plants, and are therefore sweeter. Any plant can be used to create wine, although some are much tastier to use than others.

In addition to water, sugar, and yeast, there are different chemicals that can be added to stop fermentation and make wine clearer or more stable. These do not add much to the taste of the wine but are essential to certain chemical processes that are necessary in creating a clear and clean-tasting wine.

It is the manipulation of the three essential ingredients that make each wine unique and different. Let us take a look at each of these ingredients in more detail, as they are the bases of creating any wine whether tame or wild.

Water

Water is essential to all life and it is also essential to your wine. Different regions around the world create a one-of-a-kind taste in their wine, beer, and liquor due to just the water they use. You may not think water has an actual taste, but it does. There are trace minerals that affect the taste, and they are also important for a healthy fermentation.

Not all water is created the same. There are a number of different sources for water:

- Tap water
- Spring water
- Well water
- Distilled water
- Bottled drinking water

Tap Water

As I am sure you are aware, where you live determines the source of tap water. There is a wide range of tap water, and just like Goldilocks, you must find the one that is just right.

This water is too hard

Hard water is full of minerals such as calcium, magnesium, and other metals. This type of water leaves deposits on pipes, as well as spots on dishes and kitchen utensils. You can do a simple test to determine if your water is hard. Add some water to soap or toothpaste. Hard water will not create or maintain foam very easily. Generally the pH of hard water is alkaline; this can leave a bitter taste to the water, and therefore to your wine. If you consider softening your water with a water treatment system, you should be aware that this will make the wine taste salty and unpleasant.

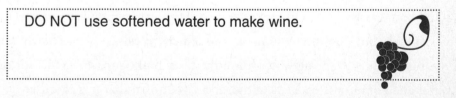

DO NOT use softened water to make wine.

You should avoid using hard water and move on to other water choices. Besides being salty, the process of softening water will remove essential minerals needed for a healthy fermentation.

This water is too soft

On the other end of the spectrum is soft water, which contains fewer minerals and the best selection if you choose to use tap water. Soft water is not perfect; it tends to be more acidic and leach metals into your wine. This can give your wine a metallic or sour taste. Taste your water first and determine if these characteristics exist before destroying a potentially good wine.

This water is just right

Relatively pH-neutral water with sufficient minerals is a good choice. You can test your water's pH at home using a water-testing kit. You can buy water-testing kits at **www.air-n-water.com**, or you can send it off to be tested at a county, state, or private lab. You can call your county's environmental agency for suggestions.

Some water supplies have a high amount of chlorine, or have been fluoridated. This can cause the taste of your wine to be off-mark. Briefly boiling your water can help release these gases without losing minerals in your water, but be careful not to over boil it. You can also pass your water through an activated charcoal filter.

Spring Water

Many homes in rural areas use spring water for their drinking water. This is the best water you can use because it contains everything you want as far as minerals, but does not contain any added chemicals, such as chlorine. If you buy gallons of spring water from the store, make sure it is really spring water and not tap water. Look at the label to confirm that it is ozonized and that it is not from a municipal water supply. Tap water from another city is not bad; it is just not really spring water. The fact that it is ozonized means no chemicals were used to kill any bacteria in the water.

Well Water

Well water is different than spring water because it often contains iron and other metals. This makes it hard water, as described above. You can try to pass it through an activated charcoal filter, but there still may be some disagreeable flavors that would not make a good choice for wine.

Distilled Water

I like to refer to distilled water as "dead water." All the water's living components and minerals are removed during the distillation process. Yeast cannot survive and populate in this kind of environment, so avoid using this type of processed water.

Bottled Water

I mentioned bottled water when discussing spring water. Many designer bottled water brands contain minerals and additives, such as salt, in an attempt to make their water more palatable. Read the labels and make sure you do not see any mention of minerals and additives and if so you should avoid them. There are some brands you can buy that do not contain a lot of additives. When I lived in a house that had bad-tasting tap water I bought the grocery store brand of spring water. It was cheap and worked wonderfully. I won three wine competitions while using that bottled water.

Never use flavored waters or fitness water. I cannot even describe what that would taste like, and it is not very likely you will ever get yeast to live in it.

When making wine from grapes, it is not as essential to add water because the fruit has plenty of liquid. In fact, water is usually used to dilute the wine if the pH or specific gravity is off; this is a "wine must." Wine must is a term that is used to describe the wine while it is fermenting. In creating wild wines, the addition of water is much more important. When you are using different parts of a plant like the stems, leaves, or even roots, they need more water to be added to the must. These parts of plants usually do not contain as much juice or water.

Sugar

Sugar is a term that can mean different types of chemical compounds. The three forms of sugar humans most often consume are glucose, fructose, and sucrose. The most common form in which sugar can be found is sucrose in a crystallized form, and is known as common white sugar. This is created from sugar cane or sugar beets. Fructose is found in fruit and corn. Glucose is a base sugar that is found in conjunction with fructose and sucrose. Beside white sugar and plant sources, sugar can also be found in high concentrations in syrups, like honey, maple syrup, or molasses.

Sugar in its natural form has a tan color and a molasses flavor. Using the more natural forms of sugar to sweeten your wine or raise the potential alcohol level will make your wine darker and give it a slight molasses taste. If you are creating a wine for your vegan friends, you may consider using raw sugar.

White sugar is processed; some sugar companies use bone char from cattle to remove the color from the sugar. This is why vegans do not eat processed sugar. Some sugar companies add activated charcoal to the process to remove the charred bone after it has bleached the sugar.

Using white sugar is fine, but be careful how much you add to wine. You can always add more sugar to wine, but you can never take any out. Using too much white sugar can impart a cidery taste to your wine.

Adding sugar to wine to increase the alcohol content and sweeten the wine is referred to as chapitalization, and there are many wine-producing areas around the world that have strict laws concerning this practice. These rules against adding sugar to sweeten wine exist in places like Italy and California. However, they are allowed to use grape juice concentrate to add sweetness. If this were a book about grape wines only, I would discourage you from adding sugar to your wine unless it was absolutely necessary. Because this is a book about wild wines, I will tell you that in some of the recipes listed the addition of sugar is an absolute necessity. Many of the ingredients in wild wines add flavor, but do not contain the same amount of sugar as grapes. It is important for both the taste of the wine and the fermentation that sugar is added.

"In order to save time/money, there have been instances where I have used excessive amounts of white table sugar in order to bump up my starting gravity. Doing this can sometimes produce an overly harsh, boozy flavor that masks the fruit."
Joe Henderkott, home winemaker

In order to stick with the theme of wild wines, let us shake things up a bit and try some different types of sugar. Here is a list of different sugars with which you may want to experiment:

Bar Sugar: This is the king of granulated sugars. It is also referred to as "ultrafine," "superfine," or, in England, as "caster sugar." In specialty food stores it is often sold as "baker's sugar."

Barbados Sugar: This is a very dark type of brown sugar. It will impart a stronger molasses flavor and darker color to your wine. It is also known as muscovado sugar.

Brown Sugar: This should not be confused with raw sugar. Brown sugar has molasses syrup added to enhance the sugar's color and flavor. The difference between light and dark brown sugar is the amount of molasses that is added to the white sugar. If you use brown sugar, it is recommended that you stick with the lighter brown sugar, as the dark brown sugar can overwhelm the flavor of your wine.

Corn Syrup: Corn syrup is mostly made of glucose and water. Some corn syrup may have other sugars, or even a vanilla flavor added to it. Make sure you read the ingredients on the label as some additives could hurt your fermentation.

Demerara Sugar: This is a type of light brown sugar, but has the consistency of large, sticky crystals. This is a premium sugar and is hard to find and rather expensive. You may want to try it in some of your recipes for a unique touch.

Dextrose: This is a type of glucose found in most fruits and honey.

Fructose: This type of sugar can be found in a variety of fruit, and is usually found paired with glucose. Fructose is much sweeter in taste than glucose, and fruits high in fructose will tend to make sweeter wines.

Galactose: This is another type of glucose and sometimes called lactose. You should not use this in winemaking as it will oxidize and form mucic acid.

Glucose: This is the other type of sugar along with fructose that is found naturally in fruit. It is fermentable but is not as sweet as fructose.

Glucose: This is the other type of sugar along with fructose that is found naturally in fruit. It is fermentable but is not as sweet as fructose.

Honey: The average composition of honey is glucose (in the form of dextrose and constitutes about 30 percent), fructose (in the form of levulose and constitutes about 38 to 40 percent), maltose (about 7 percent), and some other sugars depending on the variety. Honey may also contain water, proteins, minerals, pollens, bee parts, and other solids. The variety of honey is controlled by what flowers are available to the bees that create it. Some varieties are wildflower, locust, orange blossom, clover, and heather. There are many different varieties of honey, and they vary in color, sweetness, and composition. Honey is used as a fermentable sugar or as a sweetener in wines along with other fruits. If they are used as the primary sugar and flavor in a wine then it is referred to as mead.

Invert Sugar: This type of sugar is created through the process of changing sucrose into glucose and fructose. The forms that sugar takes when it is inverted are dextrose (a type of glucose) and levulose (type of fructose). Yeast can more readily use inverted sugar because it does not have to break down sucrose itself. You can create inverted sugar yourself by putting two parts sugar into one part water. Add two teaspoons of lemon juice per one pound of sugar (which is about two and one-fourth cups of granulated sugar). Bring this mixture to a point close to boiling for 30 minutes. Do not allow the mixture to actually boil. You should use it immediately or place it in a sealed jar in the refrigerator. Do not use the inverted sugar to sweeten wine. It might re-ferment, which as I mentioned earlier, can result in exploding bottles or a strong alcohol-tasting wine.

Jaggery: This is a type of palm sugar created in the East Indies by evaporating the fresh juice of several kinds of palm trees. It is in a raw or slightly processed form.

Maltose: This type of sugar is created from starch, specifically malt, and is processed using the amylolytic fermentation. This is the same reaction that occurs with the introduction of saliva or pancreatic juices to a starch. This can be found in small amounts in certain types of sugar and honey.

Molasses: This is the liquid part of sugar that is left after the crystallized portion has been removed. There are different grades of molasses. The lighter the grade the more sugar it contains. For instance, light molasses contains 90 percent sugar, while "blackstrap molasses" contains only 50 percent sugar and the rest is refinement residue. Because of sulfur compounds that are added to molasses, it is not usually recommended to use in winemaking because it can create an undesirable odor and flavor. There are some recipes that call for small amounts, but this is generally for a type of flavor rather than for fermentation purposes.

Piloncillo: This type is a granulated, slightly refined brown sugar from Mexico that you can buy in cone-shaped cakes. This is a more natural sugar and tastes different than other brown sugars, which have molasses added to refined sugar. Piloncillo is more like raw sugar.

Raffinose: This complex carbohydrate sugar is found in grains, legumes, and some vegetables. It is only slightly sweet, but in the wild wines it adds a distinct flavor.

Raw Sugar: This is unrefined sugar created by the evaporation of cane, beet, maple, or some other syrup. It is also known as "Sucanat." Sugar in the Raw® is one of these types of products.

Residual Sugar: This is a term to refer to the sugar that is left after fermentation has halted in a wine, which occurs one of two ways:

1. The yeast has consumed all the fermentable sugar. There may be sugar left in the wine, but this residual sugar is not fermentable.

2. The alcohol level has reached such a toxic level in the wine that the yeast dies. There may be both fermentable and non-fermentable sugars left in the wine.

Rock Candy: This type of sugar comes in large crystals made of sucrose, and is clear in color. The crystals can be tinted different colors due to flavorings added to them. Some home winemakers place a piece of rock candy in the bottom of a wine bottle before filling it, which allows the sugar to slowly dissolve and sweeten the wine.

Stachyose: This is a complex sugar that can be found in grains, legumes, and some other vegetables. It is less sweet than Raffinose, and does not work very well as a fermentable sugar or as a sweetener. It does impart a unique flavor in certain kinds of wild wines.

Sucrose: This is what regular white granulated sugar is made of and what is commonly used in winemaking. It is naturally found in grapes, fruit, and many other plants. Granulated sugar is made from refining sugar cane, sugar beets, and other sugar sources. This can be added directly to wine must. It must be broken down and inverted by the yeast into fructose and glucose before it can be used for fermentation.

Treacle: This is a refinement residue very similar to molasses; however, treacle is generally darker. "Black treacle" is very similar in taste to "blackstrap molasses." It does not contain the sulfur that molasses does, so it is much better to use in winemaking.

Experiment with sugars and see what kinds of flavors you can come up with. I would recommend you experiment in small one-gallon batches because you may be pouring a certain amount of it down the drain. You may want to try using the sugar with the fruits first in a smoothie. If you hate the combination of flavor, it will not improve much as a wine.

Yeast

Winemaking is an organic, living process rather than a set of chemical reactions that can be reproduced in a chemistry lab. There are chemical reactions that happen within the yeast cells, but it is a digestive process that cannot occur simply by mixing together chemicals. There is no way around it; you need live yeast cells to create any fermented product.

Like water and sugar, there are different types of yeast. I mentioned earlier in the book you should not use baker's yeast, the kind used to leaven bread. It will make your wine taste more like liquid bread.

Yeast live naturally on the skin of fruits such as grapes, blueberries, and plums. It is the whitish color that can often be found on wild varieties of these fruits. You can make wine by just crushing fruit and allowing the wild yeast to take over. The results are unpredictable, and you risk contamination by other microorganisms. This was the way our ancestors made wine, by stomping the fruit and allowing it to ferment naturally.

Some wild wines are created in open vats. Some wineries and brew houses have been making wine and beer for this way for centuries. Every nook, cranny, wall, floorboard, and implement in these structures contain particular strains of yeast so open vat fermentation is much easier to accomplish. The wines produced in these unique structures cannot be duplicated elsewhere, because the particular strains only exist in these places.

These little microscopic creatures live to do one thing: eat. The only food on their menu is sugar. Wine yeast usually come freeze-dried in small packets, which can be purchased from a winemaking supply store. When the must is ready, the packet is emptied into the wine mixture. The water reconstitutes them and they are ready to eat. Within a few hours they will eat, release gas, produce alcohol, and procreate. The next generation will begin to do the same as the parent yeast die off. This dead yeast sinks to the bottom of the bucket. When you make wine for the first time, you will see this ooze. This is why you rack, or take the clear wine off of the dead yeast, called lees. As you are drinking your nice Pinot Grigio, you taste yeast. They do make up the complexity to wine and actually add some protein. Picking the right yeast does matter.

There are three basic types of yeast — some for white wines, some for red wines, and others that you use for any kind of wine. There are so many different brands and variations of yeast to choose from that I have put a list of the most common types in the Appendix.

Besides dry yeast, there is also liquid yeast, which comes in two forms. The first is in what looks like a large test tube. You can shake it and dump it into your must. This is yeast in a culture, so it is already active and ready to go. You should refrigerate this until you are ready to pitch it. This slows down the yeast and keeps them fresh. You should allow liquid yeast to reach room temperature before you pitch it.

The other kind of liquid yeast is packaged in what I call a punch pack. It looks like a foil juice pack, and inside you can feel a bubble move around. This is known as a yeast activator, and inside it is the yeast. Pop the bubble by hitting it on a counter with your hand. The bubble breaks and the yeast are activated. The liquid yeast cost about $5, and dry yeast only costs about $1. The only advantage is you get a rapid, strong fermentation with liquid yeast. I have used both and can honestly say there is not much difference at the end of the day as far as the quality and the taste of the wine.

Winemaking Equipment

There is some investment that goes along with winemaking. You must be able to mix the main ingredients and store the wine must while it is fermenting. Once it is done fermenting, you must get the wine in a storage vessel, which is often a glass bottle. Finally, you must get the cork into the top of the bottle to prevent spilling and spoilage.

There is other equipment that you may wish to buy once you get the hang of your first few batches of wine, like barrels, filtering systems, crushers, and de-stemmers. Once the winemaking bug bites you, there are many different upgrades that can make winemaking easier, faster, and will allow you to produce larger quantities.

In each of the recipes in this book, you will notice one of the ingredients listed is "standard winemaking equipment." Let us begin with the pieces of equipment that are absolutely necessary in order to make the most basic wine. You could get away with a trashcan, a hose, and empty soda bottles, but the likelihood of your wine turning out bad increases dramatically. In the end of this book you will find a list of different resources where you can find winemaking supplies.

Here is the list of standard winemaking equipment:

- Primary fermentation vessel
- Secondary fermentation vessel (Carboy)
- Sanitizer
- Bottles
- Corks
- Corker

Primary Fermentation Vessel

The wine must needs somewhere to sit and ferment. There are two types of fermentation processes. I would recommend the closed fermentation system, because there is less chance of contamination.

Originally, wine was created in pottery vessels. Over time, Italians began using glass vessels called demijohns. These were placed in large baskets so they could be transported before wine bottles were used. In order to keep the wine fresh they would put a layer of olive oil over the wine. The wine was served from these vessels, and the oil floated on top and created a barrier that kept the wine from turning into vinegar. The oil did not alter the taste of the wine much because it never could really mix with it. If you have ever pulled a bottle of vinaigrette to pour on your salad, you can see the oil and vinegar are separated and you must shake hard before pouring. When the bottle is allowed to stand still, the oil will separate to the top again.

Open fermentation

Because our ancestors did not understand the concept of microorganisms, they were not sure how fermentation worked. They knew that leaving certain liquids out would change them, but to them it was a magical process. They would place crushed fruit in large, open vessels and the wild yeast would begin fermentation on its own. I am sure that many of these early batches were mostly vinegar, but over time humans discovered the existence of microorganisms, such as bacteria and yeasts.

To our ancestors, this process was so mystical they felt the secrets of fermentation belonged to the gods and goddesses of their culture. They would hold great festivals in honor of gods like Bacchus, which were celebrated for days, and sometimes weeks, during the harvest of grapes and the creation of wine. Storage techniques were still rudimentary, so the wine was quickly drunk.

An open fermentation system means the vessel where the must is fermenting is not sealed. You can use a large plastic or glass container and create wine this way. Some of my first wines were created this way, and I had some marginal success. I had a large plastic bucket and covered it with a trash bag. The bag was not used to seal it, but it did keep bugs out. It was a rather weak grape wine, and I was determined to make much better wine in the future.

I bought a fermentation bucket that looked like a large pickle barrel with a wire handle. This is what most primary fermentation vessels look like. The main criterion of a plastic wine vessel is that it must be made of food grade plastic. These can be purchased at a hardware store, a winemaking supply store, or you can also order them online. Do not use a bucket that has been used for any other purpose. If there were any chemicals stored in the bucket they can leach into your wine.

You may want to buy a bucket with a hole drilled near the bottom. The hole allows you to screw on a plastic spigot so the wine can be easily moved from one vessel to another. Most of the fermentation buckets you purchase at winemaking supply stores already have the hole. You will need a spigot to attach to the bucket and it should cost less than $5. If you buy a bucket from a hardware store, you will have to drill the hole yourself and measure it so the spigot will fit.

Bacteria, fruit flies, and other nasty bugs love open fermentation, which is why I do not recommend it. If you notice a slimy, oily slick across your wine must, it is time to dump your wine. This is what is called the "Mother." This is acetic acid bacteria, which is what creates vinegar. The more time your wine is exposed to the air, the more likely it will taste better on a salad than in a wine glass. Oxidation is another problem with open vessel fermentation. When your wine becomes oxidized, it will lose its color, turn brown, and spoil.

Some fermenters have marks on them to indicate 1-, 5-, and 6-gallon levels. If yours does not, fill the bucket with water at the different levels and mark these delineations both on the inside and outside of the bucket with a permanent marker.

Glass carboys are large bottles with a small opening that are used in wine fermentation and are not recommended for open fermentation systems, as the top opening is not wide enough to allow healthy yeast to find its way to your wine.

Closed fermentation

In order to create a closed fermentation, you will need to add a lid to your fermentation vessel. Most plastic fermentation vessels have lids that pop on top and have a rubber gasket to create an airtight seal. When you purchase a fermentation bucket from a supply store, the lid is usually included.

You should look on top of the lid to make sure you find another small hole. This is where the gas will escape. If you ever cooked with a pressure cooker, you saw the small release valve on the top. Carbon dioxide gas is released during fermentation, and without the hole you will create a gas bomb. Eventually, the pressure will pop the lid off and make a mess.

If the lid does not have a hole, many supply stores will drill the hole for you. In this hole there is a rubber ring that creates a seal for the inserted fermentation lock. The fermentation lock is another small item that will need to be purchased. It is relatively cheap, but serves a very important purpose. It allows gas to escape, but it keeps oxygen and other unwanted visitors from finding their way into your fermentation vessel. One end has a small pipe that fits into the top hole in the fermenter lid. On top is a place to put sterilized water.

When your wine is fermenting, you will see bubbles created from the carbon dioxide in your fermentation lock. It will provide you with important information. First, it will tell you when fermentation begins, and second, when it ends. You should change the water in your fermentation lock every couple of days. Make sure it is sanitized or distilled water.

> Reduce the number of times you open the lid of your fermenter. Each time you do, there is a risk of contamination.

Do not forget to place your fermentation lock on your fermenter. Imagine shaking a bottle of cola; when you open the lid the liquid comes showering out. This same thing will happen if you forget to put on your fermentation lock.

Carboy

There is another kind of fermenter that is often used, called a carboy. This is a large, glass bottle with a small neck. It works the same as a plastic bucket, except instead of a lid with a hole in it, you place a rubber stopper, or bung. These bungs are drilled with a hole so a fermentation lock can be placed into the top.

Secondary fermentation occurs after the primary fermentation ceases. Once the rapid bubbling and frothing has stopped, the wine is usually transferred to the carboy and racked off of its lees.

Secondary fermentation is often referred to as malolactic fermentation. Malolactic fermentation occurs when bacteria feed on the malic acid in the wine and turn it into lactic acid. This is a natural process, although you can add bacteria if you choose. This reduces the acidity of the wine and softens the sharpness. It mellows the wine and removes certain undesirable flavor components.

If you are making wine on a budget, you can get away with just one vessel, and do only primary fermentation, or you can use two buckets instead of a carboy. Wine will mellow over time in the bottle, but it takes longer and you risk having a lot of sediment in the bottles. These left over lees can add unpleasant flavor, and things floating in the wine might turn some off.

There is some advantage to using a carboy, and it has to do with the shape of the container. When aging wine, you want to reduce the amount of oxygen that comes in contact with your wine. Oxygen is bad because it oxidizes the wine, and can change the color and flavor of your finished product. Bad bacteria love oxygen, and can also spoil your wine in an oxygen-rich environment. Because a carboy is cone-shaped at the top it reduces the headspace in the wine. The headspace is the area between the top of your wine and the top of the vessel. One of the gasses released from wine is nitrogen, which preserves wine and prevents spoilage. When you seal your carboy, the nitrogen will naturally form a barrier, and therefore buffer your wine. It has less of an area to occupy in a carboy. The tighter you seal your carboy, the better your wine will be, because you contain the nitrogen and disallow oxygen to come into contact with your wine.

Another way to reduce headspace is to add wine or juice to your wine, depending on where you are in the process of fermentation. Evaporation occurs naturally, and you will lose a little bit of your wine when you rack it off the lees. The less headspace you leave you will have a better chance of a perfect wild wine.

There are carboys of all sizes to choose from, and there are also demijohns, which are one step bigger. In this book, I use two recipes that use a 5- to 6-gallon carboy or a 1- to 1.5-gallon carboy. The smaller carboy is essentially a small glass jug. The standard equipment includes the 5-gallon carboy, and I state whether you need a gallon carboy.

If you are making one-gallon recipes, I would recommend buying two, one-gallon carboys and using them instead of a plastic bucket. The buckets are designed to hold about six gallons of wine; a one-gallon recipe in a bucket this size will leave too much headspace. You can use one jug for primary fermentation and the second for secondary fermentation. The reason some of the recipes are for one gallon is merely for economic reasons. It takes a lot of fruit to make one gallon of wine, so a one-gallon recipe is more affordable to create than a five-gallon recipe.

When shopping for a bung to go into your carboy you must make sure it is the right size, and that it has a hole drilled into it. Most home-winemaking supply stores can help you with this. You will use the same fermentation lock that you would use with the bucket type of fermenter.

Be careful lifting your carboy. They are glass and they do not have a handle. A full carboy of wine can weigh close to 50 pounds. You should get someone to help you lift your fermenter. There will be times you will need to lift it off the ground to a higher height. When you are racking off wine into another fermenter, a siphon will only work if the carboy you are racking from is higher than the fermenter the clear wine is being siphoned into. You can buy a carboy handle that attaches to your carboy, and this will make lifting a whole lot easier.

Your fermenters are your most essential implements. There are a couple other standard items I would recommend in order to make the best wine possible. You could get away with not having these items, but you increase the risk of a bad batch of wine.

If you are having problems with your significant other not agreeing with your winemaking, the best thing to do is to include them in the process of making the wine. It should be fun and you will be glad you have an extra set of hands to help you out.

Sanitizer

"My biggest piece of advice is to keep your winemaking area and all your equipment clean and sanitized! It doesn't take much for a batch of wine to go bad, as there are always plenty of little spoilage microbes hanging around to spoil your fun."
George M. Walker, Walker Family Vintners

"Proper sanitation is one of the most important (and one of the easiest) things you can do to assure great wine. I would recommend Star San over other sanitizers."
Joe Henderkott

Repeat this mantra over and over again:

"Clean your parts before you start."

You must always clean and sanitize every piece of equipment, including your hands before coming in contact with your wine. You must sanitize every time you move your wine from one vessel to another, and your bottles must be sanitized before you fill them.

The two types of sanitizers I recommend are B-Brite and C-Brite, which come in powdered form. Dissolve a small amount of the powder in water and use the water to clean everything you are working with, including your hands. You can never sanitize something too much. The sanitizing solution will kill any bacteria or microorganisms that could hurt your wine. The great thing about these products is you do not have to rinse the equipment after you sanitize. The sanitizer will not hurt you or the wine. These products have an iodine base, which gives it killing power; but if you are sensitive to iodine, you might want to consider some other product.

Some people suggest potassium metabisulphite as a sanitizer. I would not suggest using this product to sanitize. It is used in different forms in wine, and is considered a sulfite. Sulfites occur naturally in wine in small levels. Some people cannot drink wine because they are sensitive to sulfites and using extra amounts of sulfite can cause an even greater reaction.

"You don't need to add a lot of sulfites to wine. To protect wine from spoilage beasties, 50ppm (parts per million) is plenty and does not represent 'a lot.'"
George M. Walker, Walker Family Vintners

"To prevent spoilage of my wine I like to put a carbon dioxide blanket on wine after the second racking—it keeps vinegar-producing bacteria away—they like oxygen. Using a carbon dioxide blanket also reduces the need for sulfites."
Dave Schiedermayer, home winemaker

Many people I have known with sulfite allergies have no problem drinking my wine because I do not use an excessive amount. This can shorten the shelf life of a wine, but to be honest, I have never had a batch of wine long enough for it to go bad.

I would warn against using chlorine products, as this will leave an after-taste in your wine. If you do choose to use chlorine, you should use it in diluted amounts, like one teaspoon per gallon of water. Never use soap to clean your equipment. Your wine will taste soapy because it will leave a residue on your equipment. Use the hottest water you can stand. You can even fill your dishwasher with your equipment, and instead of washing powder you can use sanitizer. This also works well for sterilizing bottles before filling them.

If you have a question about whether to sanitize it, then just sanitize it. I cannot tell you how many batches I spoiled when I first began making my own wine, simply because it became contaminated. If you ever get vinegar bacteria in your wine, the bacteria can linger in microscopic cracks and crevices. You will continue to ruin batches, and it is not worth the hassle of pouring what could be perfectly good wine down the drain because it turned to vinegar. In the long run if you ever have a batch of wine turn into vinegar, buy a new plastic fermenter and recycle your old one.

Remember your cleaning mantra; post it where near your winemaking area: You should only use your winemaking equipment for making wine. Do not use it for anything else. You should always clean and sanitize your equipment before you store it, and try to store it dry. When you use stored equipment, you will need to sanitize it again.

Bottles

You could leave the wine in a fermenter and drink it directly from there, but you would need to drink it quickly, because as the headspace grows, your wine will spoil. It would be tough to pour it from a carboy, but you could rack it back into the primary fermentation bucket and dispense it from the bottom.

> If you dispense your wine from the primary fermenter, do not forget to take off the fermentation lock. When the wine begins to pour, it creates a vacuum in the fermenter and will pull stale water from your fermentation lock into your wine.

I would recommend that you only store wine in bottles. Bottles last longer, they are easy to store, and you can keep them cool, which reduces spoilage. Keeping bottles in a cool place also reduces the chance of re-fermentation and popping bottles.

In winemaking, bottles can be the most expensive thing you will ever have to buy. You can buy them from winemaking supply stores. They are expensive to purchase online because of shipping costs.

I tell my friends that I will replace their empties with full bottles. When choosing a bottle you should use ones that do not have a screw top and ones that are colored, not clear.

You will not be able to put a cork in a screw top bottle, so you do not to save any of these types of bottles. They do not work in a corker. I recommend you be kind to the environment and recycle them. You need standard sized bottles of 750 ml, as these are the easiest to work with.

Clear bottles can spoil a wine and cause off-flavors and colors when they are struck by light. This is especially true of certain types of grain wines and meads. Wine bottles come in all different colors, so you can choose your favorite to keep or give as special gifts once you have filled them.

Wine bottles come in all shapes and sizes. The shape and size do not matter much with one exception. If you are making a sparkling or champagne-type wine, you will want to purchase champagne bottles. They are made with thicker glass because the contents will be under pressure. If you use a champagne bottle you will also need champagne stoppers and wire. If you use a regular bottle when the contents are under pressure the bottle can explode and a cork can be easily pushed out.

Ask your friends and family to save wine bottles for you. You might want to think of a place to store them because pretty soon you can be overrun with them.

For every gallon of wine you will need five 750 ml bottles. 750 ml bottles are the standard size wine bottle. For a 5-gallon batch you will need between 23-25 bottles.

If you are still having difficulty locating bottles after you have asked friends and family members, then you can ask the owners at a local bar, pub, or restaurant for their empty bottles of wine. Most of them just recycle their bottles at the end of the night, so tell them to hold them and you will pick them up. You can pick through them and recycle the bottles you do not need or cannot use. You are doing the world a favor by recycling. I bet you never thought you could be environmentally responsible by sipping homemade wild wine. You can also ask the bar owners for the boxes the wine came in. They are a great item to store empty bottles and wine.

There are two different types of winemakers: Those who care about labels stuck on used wine bottles and those who do not. I will be honest; I started off the first type and over time became the second. Here are some of the tricks I learned.

1. Heat and water. Steaming the labels or pouring hot water over them will loosen most labels, but not all. The glue used on labels today is tough. The reason they are so hard to remove is wine should last for decades and the label must last that long as well. The hotter the water, the easier it will be to get the label off.

2. Dry heat. You can use a hair drier to heat the label and try to peel it off that way. This does not work as well as using water and heat.

3. Ice. When a bottle of wine is placed in a wine bucket, the label will slip right off. You can try to put your bottles in a cooler with ice and water.

4. Try abrasive cleaner or steel wool. Rinse the bottle well after using these methods. This method can usually get off a tough label when combined with heat and water.

5. Try soaking it in water with a little ammonia or dish soap added.

6. You can soak bottles in wallpaper remover. Make sure that you rinse the bottles well before using them.

7. If you really want a clean bottle, you may need to use a razor to scratch it off. Be very careful.

> Some Web sites suggest using gasoline as a solvent. I do not think that I need to say it, but I will. Never do this. Gasoline is dangerous and has no business in home winemaking.

Later in this chapter I will discuss making your own labels. You can cover up old labels with new labels if you do not want to take the time to try to scrape them off. Scraping off wine labels is a lot of work, and I gave up. I would rather drink the wine rather than make sure the bottle looks perfect. I did make a mistake in my relinquishment, and that was I did not bother to label the bottles in any discernable way. This became a problem because when I made more than one batch of wine, I forgot which bottle contained a particular wine.

Mark the top of your corks — just remember what your scrawl means six months later. I homebrew beer as well, which is a similar process to making wine. I made the mistake of not labeling the bottles when I brewed two beers at the same time. One beer was a Canadian beer and one was a Mexican-style beer. I decided that the Canadian beer tasted like Molsen and the Mexican tasted like Corona beer. So, I put either a "C" or an "M" on the tops of the beer caps. At the time is seemed like pure genius, but a couple of months later I looked at the caps and thought to myself, "What does the C and M stand for? Do they represent Mexican and Canadian or do they mean Molsen and Corona?" Not one of my brighter moments, but in the end I just put them all in an ice bucket and invited friends over. The beer disappeared and no one really cared.

Learn your lesson on labeling bottles. It is best to include some type of label. It does not have to be fancy; it just has to say what it is in it.

> For all of you beer home brewers, I have heard the question whether a wine can be stored in beer bottles with a cap. I believe that capping a wine in a beer bottle is acceptable. I would not store it for a long period of time in beer bottles if I were trying to age a wine. Wine is acidic and can be corrosive; therefore, placing it in a bottle with a metal cap for a long period of time could lead to a rusty wine.

Corks

If you have bottles you must find a way to seal them; corks nicely do the job. They expand when in a bottle and seal the wine from the outside world and any bacteria that could spoil your wine. The bad news is corks are not reusable. Once they are removed they need to be tossed, although you could mulch them or recycle them as wood.

Corks come in different sizes, just like bottles. Make sure you buy the right sized corks for the bottles you are using or they may not fit correctly. For those who are eco-conscious, corks come from a type of tree that is becoming endangered. The rate of use is greater than replanting rates. Many wine companies have gone to using rubber synthetic corks. These are a fine choice and I have not noticed a difference in the taste or color of wine that has a synthetic cork. For those purists who believe corks allow wines to breathe, synthetic corks are evil.

There is a danger in using corks: "cork taint." It is caused by a chemical called TCA (2,4,6-trichloroanisole), which is created by fungus that lives in cork fiber. It totally ruins the taste of a wine, should you use infected corks. Soak corks in sanitizer before you cork the bottle with them. This also creates a better seal on the bottle. Do not soak them too long because the cork can swell and make it harder to insert into the bottle. You should limited soaking to about ten minutes. Make sure the corks you are trying to use are long, straight corks. Do not use tapered corks.

Corker

You could try all day, but you will never be able to push a cork all the way into a bottle by hand. You will need a corker. The most basic and least expensive corker is a hand corker. It takes some hand strength because you need to compress the cork by squeezing it together before pushing it in with a plunger. Hand corkers work best with cheaper compressed corks. They do not work to well with natural or synthetic corks because they are too hard to compress. You are better off using a floor corker, described in the next section.

Be sure the corks are inserted all the way into the bottle. This is where friends and family can help. You may need someone with upper arm power to do it, or at least have someone hold the bottle. It is best to have the bottle on the ground rather than on a tabletop to prevent it from slipping.

This ends the list of essentials. The next two sections discuss upgrades and other implements that will make your winemaking world a happy and harmonious place. Most of the items in this first section can be bought together as a winemaking kit from a home-winemaking supplier. You can often buy a kit for less than what it would cost to buy the pieces individually. You might also consider buying a wine concentrate kit to try out first. These kits come with all of the ingredients to make five gallons of wine. Everything is measured out and included. There are detailed instructions and unless you are not paying attention or fail to follow the cleaning mantra, you should be able to create a great wine the first time you try it.

Intermediate Supplies

"I recommend shopping on the Internet. Most winemaking supply shops have Internet storefronts and many offer discounts or deals for buying from the Web. There are many of these stores throughout the country. Although I have a good store not far from me, I still shop on the Internet to ensure I'm getting the best selection and best pricing. I have had one problem on eBay: I bought a couple oak barrels that did not work properly."
George M. Walker, Walker Family Vintners

There is some equipment you can immediately upgrade. These are not serious upgrades like the list in the advanced section; rather, they are small items that can allow you to control the results of your winemaking and make some of the actions much easier. These are not usually included in beginner home winemaker kits, unless you are lucky.

Here is a list of intermediate supplies:

- Bottle brushes
- Bottle filler
- Hydrometer
- Floating thermometer
- Wine spoon
- Tubing
- Clarifier/stabilizer
- Acids
- Other additives

Bottle Brushes

In order to clean bottles and carboys, you can buy bottle brushes. Both bottles and carboys can have sediment that forms on the bottom and can be hard to shake loose with just simple rinsing. Bottle brushes come in different sizes. You can buy the smaller one for your bottles and the long large ones for your carboy. You can bend the handle slightly on the long brush before inserting into your carboy so you can reach all the nooks and crannies. The bend is especially helpful in cleaning the upper part of the carboy.

Use the bottle brush on the bottles, especially if they are used bottles, before you sanitize them. Use hot water and fill the wine bottle. Use the brush to clean the bottle of any sediment. Hold the bottle up to a bright light so you are sure you cleaned everything. If you leave sediment you are asking for trouble later on.

After using your carboy in fermentation, fill the carboy about a quarter full of hot water and use the brush to clean the bottom and the sides. Without a brush this is almost impossible unless you fill the carboy with hot water and let it soak an hour or more. Even then you will have difficulty.

Do not use your brush on a plastic primary fermenter. Brushes can cause scratches in the plastic, which is a great place for microorganisms to hide. In fact, you should never use any kind of abrasive on a plastic fermenter.

Bottle Filler

A bottle filler, in some ways, belongs in the essentials list. You can get by without having one, but once you have one you will wonder why you did not buy it earlier. When filling bottles from a fermenter, you must manually cut off the flow.

The bottle filler fits on the end of the tubing, which you can read about below. It is a long plastic pipe that fits into the wine bottle. At the end of the pipe is a spring mechanism. When you push the pipe down it allows the wine to flow. When you release the pressure, the flow stops. I would still recommend that you place something on the floor (like an old towel) beneath your wine bottles, as you will have some spillage.

From past experience, I would recommend wearing special winemaking clothes. Wine stains and juice are sticky. One time, I was wearing a relatively new pair of leather shoes and was making mead, and somehow honey dripped on the top of these shoes. The shoes were ruined and my wife was not happy. Every time she saw me getting ready to make wine or mead, she told me to put on my honey shoes. These shoes became the official winemaking loafers.

The other function of the bottle filler is to create headspace. Up to now I have said that headspace is bad, but in the case of bottles, a little headspace is necessary. Look at any commercial wine. You will see a space between the top of the liquid and the cork. This is to allow some off gassing of the wine. Wine will release some gasses while it is in the bottle. If you do not allow some room then the gases will make room by pushing your cork right out of the bottle. Have you ever heard a popgun? That is the sound you will hear, and it is a matter of physics. The bottle filler takes up some room in the bottle when it is inserted. Even if you fill the bottle to the top with wine, when you remove the filler there will be some space left in the bottle. It is the perfect amount of headspace. Trust me: you do not want to recreate Old Faithful. It is better to drink wine than to try to figure how to get it off the ceiling.

Bottle fillers usually cost less than $20. It might be a good idea to buy one early in order to save time, mess-cleanup, and aggravation.

Hydrometer

At the beginning of all of the recipes, you will see the letters OG and FG. OG stands for Original Gravity and FG represents Final Gravity. These letters are followed by a number and are important because they lead to the ABV or alcohol by volume. Remember that yeast eats sugar and converts it into alcohol. The amount of fermentable sugar in a wine will determine how much alcohol a certain wine should contain when it has finished fermenting. Another abbreviations you will see is SG or Specific Gravity. This is the same measurement as OG and FG.

This is important to know for a couple of reasons. First, when you are fixing your wine at the beginning and preparing it for fermentation, knowing the OG will help you determine if you need any more sugar or if the mixture needs a little dilution. Knowing the final gravity will help you determine when fermentation is over. If the wine has not quite reached the final gravity, it could mean your fermentation is stuck, you picked the wrong kind of yeast, or that it is still quietly fermenting. Bottling the wine too soon could make it too sweet, or it will not have enough alcohol for taste, or it could continue to ferment in the bottle.

In order to understand specific gravity, think in terms of density. You can try this little experiment to understand how this works.

1. Fill a wine bottle to the top with water.
2. Place an unsharpened pencil, eraser side down, into the water. It will float.
3. Mark on the pencil where the top of the bottle is.
4. Empty the water into a container and add a cup of sugar to it. Mix it well until the sugar dissolves.
5. Fill the bottle with the sugar water.
6. Place the pencil, eraser-side-down, into the liquid. You will notice the line you marked on the pencil the first time is higher above the water line. This is because the mixture of water and sugar is denser than just plain water.

The pencil you used in the experiment is a crude but effective hydrometer. Wine hydrometers are sealed glass tubes with a paper label inside them. In the bottom is usually mercury or some other heavy metal to weigh it down, just like the eraser. There are usually three different scales, but the one that shows specific gravity is the one that has 1.000 on it and numbers above and below 1.000. This number 1.000 is the specific gravity of plain water. The numbers below the 1.000 are higher, and this is because liquids that show this reading are denser than water. The numbers above the 1.000 on the scale like, .999, are less dense than water. Alcohol is less dense than water. You could repeat the pencil experiment and pour rubbing alcohol into the bottle. I will save you the trouble and show that the pencil will sink lower than the line for plain water.

On many hydrometers there are two other scales. These scales are Balling Scale or "Brix." They are measurements of the potential alcohol of your wine. The Brix scale shows you how much sugar there is in a liquid. In order to use the potential alcohol content you can do a reading of the potential alcohol before it ferments and then after it is finished. Then subtract the two numbers. All three of these scales use the same process of determining what the specific gravity of a liquid is, but each scale is just another way of reading it. It is similar to a thermometer that has Fahrenheit and Celsius scales. These are both measurements of the same level of mercury.

So if it is 10 percent before and 4 percent after, the potential alcohol content of your wine is about 6 percent. The reason this works is because the sugar was converted to alcohol and the amount of change in gravity is alcohol replacing the sugar. This potential alcohol is the same as the ABV number on the recipe. The Balling reading shows how much sugar is in the mixture. It is assumed your must is denser because of the amount of sugar in it. When you are finished making the wine your Balling will be lower.

You really just need to concentrate on the specific gravity. If you want to try to figure out what the alcohol content will be before you make a wine, and only have OG and FG, you can use this formula.

$$\text{Approximate Alcohol Content (\%)} = \frac{FG \quad - \quad OG}{0.0074}$$

I have made it easy for you and already calculated the ABV in each recipe. It is important to know the potential alcohol content of a wine because it will help you decide which yeast to use. Please note that the recipes in this book has estimates; there may be varying results based upon whether the wine is sweeter or drier, the type of yeast you use and other variables that are hard to control in a home environment. The gravities provided should be used as a general goal, not to be used in a strict way. The best way to determine your gravity is to take hydrometer readings throughout the process of winemaking. Use your palate and nose as well; remember to trust your instincts. Winemaking at home is more of an art and hobby rather than a hard science.

If your wine has a potential alcohol content of 18 percent, but you are using yeast that dies out at 14 percent, then you will end up with a sweet wine with less alcohol. You may desire less alcohol in your wine, but alcohol does significantly contribute to the overall taste of a wine. Having too much or too little alcohol can make a wine either weak or overpowering.

Be aware that temperature can alter a hydrometer reading. Try to read a hydrometer at room temperature. If it is too cool or hot, your reading can be off because liquid contracts when it gets hot and becomes denser when it cools.

You should also purchase a hydrometer-testing jar. This makes it easier to read and uses only a small amount of wine. You should always clean your equipment after use, but never return a wine sample back into the fermenter. You can taste it if you like and dump the rest when you are done. I have found that tasting the wine during the different stages of fermentation has helped me learn what it should taste and smell like. This helps me determine when a wine is done or when there is a problem going on that needs to be fixed.

When testing to see if a wine has stopped fermenting you should not just rely on one reading. Test it over a couple of days and if the reading remains constant then it has stopped. If it is still changing you should wait until it has completely stopped fermenting before you consider bottling the wine.

Floating Thermometer

The temperature of your wine is very important for fermentation and for aging. If your wine is too hot or too cold the yeast will die off or go into a suspended state. If you kill the yeast you will have to start all over again. When aging a wine you want it cool so things can settle down and refermentation does not reoccur.

°F Adjust   40 - .002
50 - .001
60
70 + .001
80 + .002
90 + .004
100 + .005
110 + .007
120 + .008
130 + .010
140 + .013
150 + .015

If you could dedicate a temperature-controlled room for winemaking, this would be great. Most people must use their kitchen, bathroom, garage, or outbuilding for their hobby. These areas are a little harder to control the temperature in.

Before pitching the yeast into a wine must you must make sure it is as close to room temperature as possible, or maybe a little above. Do not pitch the yeast above 75 degrees Fahrenheit. If you can keep the must at about 68 degrees Fahrenheit during primary fermentation, this is a good temperature for healthy yeast growth. If you drop below 60 degrees your yeast will go dormant.

I have found that floating thermometers work the best for testing wine. You can place them in the fermenter to take a direct reading. The other time to check the temperature is before taking a hydrometer reading for as accurate a reading as possible.

The fact that the thermometer floats makes it easy to read and retrieve. I recommend tying a monofilament string on the top loop so your hand does not go anywhere near the must. Remember to sanitize the thermometer every time you use it.

If your must is not the right temperature, here are some suggestions.

- Buy a Brew Belt or a FermaWrap heater. These wrap around the fermenter and allow you adjust the heat of the must. The FermaWrap will work on a plastic bucket or a carboy. A Brew Belt is not recommended for use on a glass carboy. They are less than $30 and plug into the wall.

- Wrap the fermenter in a blanket. Do not use an electric blanket because it is not safe.

- Wrap insulation around your fermenter. It will keep the must at a constant temperature. The problem I have found with this is that it gets ruined if it gets wet.

- Wrap it in foam rubber. This works similar to insulation but it can get wet and be washed.

- If it is too hot, place the fermenter in an ice bath. This will cool it quickly and is not recommended for use during rapid fermentation.

- Place in a basement or springhouse. These places are cool and have a constant temperature. These are good places for aging your wine.

- Place a wet T-shirt over your fermenter and place a fan next to it. This is a homemade air conditioning system. This will cool it quickly and is not recommended during fermentation.

- If you have to heat a liquid such as water to dissolve honey in mead, you can use what is called a wort chiller. This is usually used for brewing beer, but will work with a wine or mead as well. It is copper tubing that is inserted into the liquid and cold water runs through it. The heat from the liquid is transferred out of the liquid with the flowing water. This is a quick way to drop the temperature in order to get it close to the temperature needed to pitch the yeast.

> "The best place to ferment wine is in a warm but-not-too-warm environment for reds, a cool but-not-too-cool environment for whites. A home basement is just about perfect for both."
>
> *George M. Walker, home winemaker*

Wine Spoon

Earlier I mentioned you should eventually have equipment used for winemaking and no other tasks. You do not want to use the same spoon that you used to stir last night's chili. You can purchase a wine spoon that has a long handle, which is usually made from plastic or stainless steel. You should not use a wooden spoon because bacteria can hide in the pores, no matter how much you clean it. Of the two options I would recommend the stainless steel because the plastic spoon can get scratches that can hide bacteria. You can purchase one from a winemaking supplier. They are usually long enough to stir must in a fermenter and are easy to clean and sterilize. You can use a spoon for the following activities:

- Stir in yeast when you pitch it into the must.
- Stir and mix wine ingredients.
- If you need to heat any ingredients on the stove you will need to stir so it does not burn.

- You should stir a must to aerate it for yeast to begin fermenting.
- Stir and dissolve sugar or honey in a must.
- Remove fruit, cheesecloth, or bag from the fermentation vessel.
- See if you can balance it on your nose and impress your friends.

Tubing

There is a number of beginning winemaking kits that include tubing. You will find that it is almost essential in transferring wine to another vessel, and is needed for transferring wine into bottles. This is one item you can buy from the hardware store. You need to measure the diameter of your spigot and bottle filler before you purchase it. Also, make sure that it is food grade flexible tubing. It is relatively cheap, so buy it by the yard. It is an item that is very difficult to clean, so if there is any buildup, you should recycle it and cut a new piece of tubing.

Before cutting the tubing, measure how much you will need to go from the fermenter to a bottle or another fermenter. Once you cut it, you cannot tape it back together, so take the time to measure it first. You can have a couple of different sets of tubing in order to use them for different tasks.

Before using the tubing, fill a container with sanitizer and soak the tubing. Then run hot water through the tubing. After using the tubing, repeat this process and make sure there is not water in the tube. Hang it up to dry.

"My advice for a beginning winemaker is to find a veteran home winemaker to help coach. Just make sure he or she knows what they're doing! Otherwise, do a little reading on home winemaking to learn the terminology and processes. Beyond that, just jump in and don't give up if your first batch isn't everything you hoped it would be. Practice makes perfect."
George M. Walker, Walker Family Vintners

Clarifiers/Stabilizers

Clarifiers are additives that help clear your wine and stabilizers stop the fermentation process and prevent the growth of other microorganisms. I recommend you have some of these on hand. Here is a list of some clarifiers:

- Bentonite
- Sparkolloid
- Isinglass
- Kitisol 40
- Pectic Enzyme (This is very important for many fruit wines)

Some common stabilizers are:

- Potassium Metabisulfite Powder
- Campden Tablet (compressed form of Potassium Metabisulfite)
- Potassium Sorbate

Acids

You can purchase acids separately as citric, ascorbic, malic, and tartaric acid. I would recommend an acid blend instead. A blend consists of 67 percent tartaric acid and 33 percent malic acid. There are chemicals that reduce the level of acid in a wine, such as calcium carbonate and potassium bicarbonate. Each of these cost a few dollars. Before adding these to a wine, I recommend you buy a pH and acid testing kit. You can read about these below in the advanced supplies.

Other Additives

You can add yet more chemicals to your wine. You might consider adding a water conditioner if you have hard water such as gypsum or Burton salts. These additives condition the water without hurting the flavor of your wine.

In order to help your yeast out, you can add yeast nutrient and yeast energizer. Each of these can help a stuck or slow fermentation. Each of these additives cost only a few dollars. Before adding any of these you should question whether you really need them as some of them have the potential to add odd flavors.

> I have found that plain gelatin or an egg white work well as a clarifier in a pinch.

Advanced Supplies

Are you ready to upgrade? Are you a "gear" junkie like me? In this section I will offer you a list of equipment that is either an upgrade of your current equipment or is additional equipment that can help you in your quest to make bigger and wilder wine.

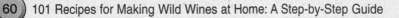

Here is a list of upgrades and wine gear:

- Floor corker
- Larger fermenter
- Pail opening tool
- Carboy wedge
- Filtration system
- Crusher/De-stemmer
- Wine press
- Bottle washer
- Bottle tree
- Barrels
- Juicers/Pitters
- Pump transferors
- Siphon
- Funnels/Strainers
- Pulp bags
- Upgrade faucets
- Collapsible jug
- ph testing kit/ Sulphite tester
- Alcohol tester
- Fancy labels
- Foils

Floor/Bench Corker

Is your hand and back tired yet from forcing corks into bottles? There is an easier way. A bench and a floor corker work the same way. One can sit on your counter and the other is tall and can be used on the floor. Many of these come from Italy and have a durable design, so you will never have to replace them. You can cork up to about

150 bottles an hour. It is a lock and load method. Drop a cork in the top and put the bottle snuggly underneath. Pull down the arm and the bottle is perfectly corked without any damage. Sometimes you can end up butchering corks using a hand unit. If you find you want to use synthetic corks or you are creating a lot of five-gallon batches, then this is well worth the investment. These units sell for around $100.

Larger Fermenter

You can buy larger carboys and demijohns up to 15-gallon sizes. These are very heavy and are not very portable or practical. I would recommend considering other types of primary fermenters.

There are screw-on lid plastic fermenters. If you ever had to get a lid off a primary fermenter, you will know that this can be very difficult. These buckets have the spigot and airlock.

You can go up to stainless steel units. These can run a few hundred dollars and can hold up to 30 gallons of wine. The nice thing is that it has an inflatable gasket that allows you to brew any amount of wine because it allows you to adjust the level of the lid. These units run about $500, and are not generally very mobile.

You do have another option, and that is a larger plastic fermenter. This is more like the stainless steel fermenters that you find in wineries, only smaller. They have many extras added on and, like the stainless steel varieties, can hold large volumes of wine.

> "We use 55-gallon food-grade plastic barrels. We now make anywhere from 300 to 350 gallons each year through our cooperative."
> *George M. Walker, Walker Family Vintners*

Pail-Opening Tool

This can make getting the lid off a plastic fermenter much easier. It is a metal hand tool that can get up and under the lid and save your fingers from getting hurt trying to pry off the lid. This lifesaving device goes for about $5. I have one and cannot live without it.

Filtration System

> "White and Rosé should be filtered. With these, the sparkle and the clarity are a big part of the drinking experience. With reds, it's up to you. I like unfiltered red."
> *Chris Minnick, home winemaker*

There are different levels of filtering from the reasonable to the extremely expensive. The cheapest way to filter your wine is to use coffee filters in a funnel. Filtering is not a necessity for most amateur home winemakers. It is more of a matter of aesthetics, if you are opposed to any kind of sediment in the bottom of the bottle once a wine has settled.

There are a number of clarifiers mentioned in the last section. If you can be patient, most wine will clear on its own. If you do want a filtering system, expect to pay between $50 and $500. The lower end of a filter system is a gravity-fed kind that uses disposable filters. This works great for one-gallon batches, but for anything larger than that is gets clogged and you end up using multiple filters for one batch.

The next step up is a pressure system you can hand pump. This works better than the gravity-fed and can clear much larger batches up to ten gallons. This costs about $100.

You then get into the much more expensive jet models. These have electric pumps that force the wine through a number of filters. This will produce very clear wine, but for me it is just not worth the expense.

> "Filtering is an additional process that will certainly yield a cleaner, more sparkling wine and one that is less likely to re-ferment in the bottle or to develop sediment of a few kinds. However, in my opinion, unless you're into putting all that extra work into your winemaking, it's just not necessary. Most red wines will clear very well over just a few months of settling and a racking or two. Whites are more problematic, since there is potential for solids to drop out due to changes in the environmental temperature. Therefore, filtering will help, but you will also need a first step of stabilizing the white wine (using cold or hot methods) prior to filtering it."
>
> *George M. Walker, Walker Family Vintners*

> "I don't filter my wine; instead I rely on multiple fermentation cycles to achieve clarity."
>
> *Joe Henderkott*

Crusher/De-stemmer

You can buy crushers that are not de-stemmers. A de-stemmer is mostly for those who want to create grape wines. Fruit crushers can be hand cranked or motorized. They are very similar to a wood chipper in that they grind the fruit with rotating teeth. This prepares the fruit to be pressed. These range from $200 to $400. A de-stemmer can run about $500.

Wine Press

The most common fruit presses are the ratchet and screw types. They have a plate that moves down on the fruit when you pump the ratchet or turn the screw wheel. Some presses have a bladder that gently crushes the fruit without extracting bitter flavors from the seeds and tannins.

You can buy a small tabletop press for one to five gallons of wine for about $130 and the other larger screw-and-ratchet models run upward of $500. A bladder press can run thousands of dollars.

Bottle Washer

This is a piece of equipment that can screw onto your faucet where you clean your bottles and carboy. It puts the water under pressure to clean better and it has a push trigger that only releases water when you press your bottle or carboy onto it.

Bottle Tree

This is a quick way to sanitize and store bottles. It is a tower where you place your bottle on branches that stick out. This keeps the bottle upside down to dry and keeps them cleaner. Some models have an attachment that will spray sanitizer up into the bottles before you hang them.

Barrels

There are three main types of oak barrels you can buy to age your wine: American, Hungarian, and French. They come in different sizes, but they can be expensive. Be careful buying any used barrels, as they can leak. If you are purchasing a new oak barrel, one of the things you will be asked is what level of toasting you want. This is similar to roasting coffee. The inside of the barrel is toasted to different levels of char. This imparts different amounts of oak flavor to your wine. Oak barrels range from $200 to more than $500 per barrel. They do not last forever and can wear out and leak.

There are alternatives, such as liquid oak and oak chips that can be added to the wine. The oak chips are allowed to soak in an aging wine and then are removed. The chips often come from used barrels that have been broken down. This imparts a decent oak flavoring without the oak barrel price.

Juicers/Pitters

These tools are great for the wild wine maker. A steam juicer uses hot water to extract juice from fruit. This makes extraction easy without the need to crush and press. A steam juicer costs about $200. A pitter is great for getting pits out of cherries or similar fruit, and can cost about $40.

Transfer Pumps

These pump wine from one vessel to another quickly. These are electrical units that can pump one to three gallons a minute and come with a price tag of about $200.

Siphon

These are a much cheaper alternative to a pump. A wine siphon is a long tube within a tube that, when depressed, starts wine moving from one vessel to another. These run less than $20 and I cannot live without mine. The alternative is sucking the wine through the tube to start the wine flowing. Not the most sanitary way to move wine.

Funnels/Strainers

Funnels come in all shapes and sizes. Some have strainers that will fit inside. They can catch large particles as wine passes through. It is a nice alternative to filtering and can catch pulp and pits from fruit. These cost less than $10, including the filter screen that is washable and reusable.

Pulp Bags

If you are tired of trying to use cheesecloth to place fruit in when making wine, you can buy a nylon bag to put your fruit pulp in. They are convenient because they are washable and reusable. They cost less than $20 and come in different sizes.

Upgrade Faucets

You can change the faucet on your fermenters to a high-flow lever faucet. You may even consider an inline faucet. This can be placed between two pieces of tubing and give you control over the flow. Each of these only cost a few dollars.

Collapsible Jug

This is just what it sounds like. These are plastic jugs that can be folded up when you are finished with them. They are great for home winemakers that have limited room to do their hobby and need to save on storage space. This is the type of fermenter I started with and they work fine. They cost about $10. This is great for the home winemaker on a budget.

pH Testing Kit/Sulphite Tester

There are a number of test kits for your inner chemist. These use different solutions and papers to test the amount of acid or the amount of sulfite in your wine. There are kits to test malic acid, residual sugar, and lactic acid. I love to fool around with these kits, but if you follow the recipes closely you will not really need to use them. Your taste buds and nose are your best testers. Drink what you like and dump the rest.

CASE STUDY: JOE HENDERKOTT

Westfield, IN
Home Winemaker

I've been a home winemaker and brewer for about three years. I enjoy creating something totally from scratch and watching it evolve into something wonderful. It also gives me a chance to be creative and produce something that may not be readily available commercially. I started my home brewing adventures after helping a friend brew beer. I eventually moved on to making my own wine at home.

My favorite grape wine is a Syrah. They are spicy and earthy but can still have strong fruit notes that go very well with food. My favorite wild wine is mead. Meads can be served using straight honey or can be combined with fruits (melomel), wine (pyment), herbs and spices (metheglin), or grain (braggot) to create a broad spectrum of flavors.

I've gone through **www.northernbrewer.com**, Great Fermentations of Indiana, and local hardware and grocery stores to buy supplies for winemaking. If I were to suggest a beginning winemaking kit it would include the following:

- 6.5-gallon brew bucket or carboy
- five-gallon carboy
- Bung and airlocks
- Auto siphon
- Siphon hose
- Bottle filler
- 24 wine bottles

Here are some non-essentials that I recommend you buy when you can:

- Wine thief
- Brew pot
- Carboy brush
- Mash paddle

From my experience I recommend that you ferment your wine in a cool, dark place that will maintain a relatively constant temperature over long periods of time. Also make sure it is in a location where it will not need to be moved much.

CASE STUDY: JOE HENDERKOTT

The most ideal locations include your basement or a closet. I try not to ferment in my garage as the temperature can change much more drastically than indoors. I also avoid places near large windows as the sunlight can damage the wine.

I began by using glass carboys (6.5-, 5-, and 3-gallons vessels) but have since moved to Better Bottles, which are food grade PET. I have read too many horror stories to continue using glass.

Here are some places I would recommend if you would like to taste some commercially made wild wines.

Thomas Family Winery produces Gale's Hard Cider
208 E Second Street
Madison, IN 47250
www.thomasfamilywinery.us

New Day Meadery
701 South Anderson Street
Elwood, IN 46036
www.newdaymeadery.com

After primary fermentation I've sometimes moved my wine to secondary vessels, which are too large. The added headspace has allowed oxygen to mix with the wine and produce off-flavors.

–Joe Henderkott

Here are some food-pairing suggestions for wild wines:
- Roast chicken and cider
- Chocolate cake with blackberry mead
- Cheesecake and Lambic (not a wild wine per se but it does use wild fruits)

Grape Wines

You would not start stunt driving the first time you got behind the wheel of
a car, and you cannot begin creating wild wines without getting the basics
of winemaking down first. This is not like driving school. The basic wines
you create will be tasty and you will be the envy of all your friends.

The principles are simple and once you master the basics of winemaking,
you can create any wine you wish and experiment with different ingredients. Keep in mind that almost any plant can be turned into a wine. Some

are better choices than others. I would suggest that if you would not eat the ingredient in its natural form, I would not recommend the time and expense of creating a wine from it.

As I have mentioned in earlier chapters the basic components are simple — water, yeast, and a sugar source. All the other ingredients either make the wine taste better or clear the wine and make it look better.

There are many different techniques represented in this book. Some use yeast energizer and nutrients while others may not. These recipes have been tried and have produced wine that is palatable. If you want to add any other ingredients that will clarify or add to the taste of the wine, I would encourage you to do so. There is no right or wrong way to make wine, other than it has to contain the three major components in the right proportion and that you always use clean technique when creating the wine. This is a natural process that occurs every day in nature. This book just helps you push the ingredients in the right direction to produce wine that is consistent in taste and presentation.

The first recipe I offer you here is proof. It will not necessarily make award-winning wine, but it will make a nice, sweet wine that you can easily share with friends and family.

I grew up a Catholic, and this wine reminds me a lot of the wine used as sacramental wine. The type of grapes used in this recipe is the exception to my earlier statement about wine grapes being different from eating grapes. Most brands of frozen grape juice are made from concord grapes. They are sweet and have a definite memorable taste. These are the types of grapes that are used in grape jelly as well.

Back to the Basics

Ingredients:

- 24 oz frozen grape juice concentrate
- 1 gallon water

- 3 cups granulated sugar
- 1 packet wine yeast
- Primary fermentation bucket
- Gallon jug (carboy)

Instructions:

1. Defrost grape juice concentrate to room temperature. Add concentrate and water to carboy. Stir and dissolve sugar into the mixture. Cover and let sit for 24 hours.

2. Add yeast and attach airlock. Allow fermenting for three weeks.

3. Rack clear wine off the sediment*

4. Bottle wine. This wine does not age well, so drink right away.

You can try this same simple recipe with any frozen juice concentrate.

Racking simply means siphoning clear wine off of the sediment in a fermenter into a secondary fermenter.

Grape Varietals

There are thousands of different grape varieties, and these are called varietals. These are used to create simple wines. There are many wines that are blended. Winemakers blend wine in order to improve the taste.

Every year's crop produces a different grape, and the same grapes can differ according to where they are grown. Some of these areas are referred to as appellations. In France certain wines can only come from certain appellations.

The vintage of a wine has to do with the year the grapes that are picked. This is important to know because a wine can be aged for a long time before it is bottled, but the vintage is the year the grapes were harvested.

A vintage in a certain vineyard can vary year to year. Some years are better than others, due to disease, weather, and pests. Many wineries will blend different vintages of a wine to make sure their wine is consistent from year to year. Another type of blending is when a vintner takes different varietals and creates a new wine. This is a fascinating art of taking very different flavored wines and creating a new flavor.

Most of the wines in this book use only one fruit or ingredient. You may want to try blending some of your wines when you have a few different varieties on hand. Experiment with small portions of each before you dump them all in a large bucket. Take your time and take notes.

Red Wine Recipe

I am including a simple red wine recipe. The recipe is using grapes rather than grape concentrate. There are plenty of wine kits you can buy that will give you experience working with wine concentrates. You will be creating wild wines, which means you will be handling actual fruits and other natural ingredients. In this recipe I will go into more detail than in other recipes. This is to give you an idea of how to create a wild wine step by step. Once you get the hang of it here, you will not need complete instructions every time.

Here is a list of some common red wine varietals:

- Cabernet Sauvignon
- Pinot Noir
- Zinfandel
- Merlot
- Cabernet Franc
- Petite Sirah
- Syrah
- Shiraz
- Sangiovese
- Malbec
- Grenache

This is by no means a complete list, but it is the most common types of red wine grapes you are likely to encounter.

Through the next few chapters you will find a number of recipes categorized according to the primary plant that is used as the flavoring source for the wine. Not all plants have enough sugar to produce a wine, so sugar or honey must be added in order for the wine to ferment.

Each recipe will begin with how much wine the recipe will make. This will be either one or five gallons. You can adjust the one-gallon recipes in order to make more wine, but it is not recommended that you try to break down a five-gallon recipe in order to make less wine, as the proportions may not allow for less to be made.

You will then notice OG (original gravity), FG (final gravity), and ABV (alcohol by volume). These values are to help you have a target to move toward. Your particular wine may not fall exactly on these numbers but it should fit closely in the range. The best way to determine what the readings are is to take them with a hydrometer and make notes as you go along. It should be noted that drier wines will have a lower Final Gravity because there is less residual sugar in the wine. Also you should sweeten wine using your palate. Take it slowly, and only add small amounts of sugar as you can always add more sugar, but you cannot take any away.

The next part of the recipe is the ingredients. This is everything you will need to create your wild wine. In addition you will see "standard winemaking equipment." You can find a list of what equipment you will need in Chapter 1. If there is additional equipment, such as a smaller carboy or a nylon bag, it will be listed under ingredients. It is recommended that you have all of your ingredients and equipment ready and sanitized before you start. You should read each recipe thoroughly as there may be pre-steps such as freezing fruit that has to be done a day or two before you start the actual process of winemaking.

Under the instructions section you will find simple step-by-step instructions. For this first recipe I have written out more detailed instructions. You can refer back to these. The recipes are not as detailed. You may decide to condition your water, or add clarifiers at the end.

Cabernet Sauvignon

Yield 1 gallon/3.8 L

OG = 1.100 FG = .995 ABV = 14 %

Ingredients:

- 12 lbs Cabernet Sauvignon grapes
- 3 ½ lbs of sugar
- 3 campden tablets
- 1 tsp yeast nutrient
- 1 packet wine yeast
- 2 tsp pectic enzyme
- Water
- Standard winemaking equipment
- Nylon bag/Cheesecloth
- 1 Gallon carboy

> "The biggest mistake you ever made making wine was buying too many poor-quality grapes because the price was right."
> *Chris Minnick, home winemaker*

Instructions:

These instructions will assume that you have basic winemaking equipment and not expensive equipment such as a crusher or de-stemmer. Therefore these directions allow you to create a wine from fruit by hand. If you are lucky enough to access more sophisticated equipment then the process will be easier and take less time.

Although more sophisticated equipment is nice to have, it is not necessary. Because most of the recipes in this book are one-gallon or five-gallon recipes, you should have no difficulty preparing the ingredients by hand or using common kitchen appliances.

Day One:

You will need to purchase or pick wine grapes. Regular eating grapes are not normally fit for making wine. They do not contain enough tannin and the skins are too thin. The exception is concord grapes that I mentioned in the basic recipe. You can buy wine grapes from farmer's markets or from local vineyards. It takes about 12 pounds of grapes to produce a gallon of wine. If you cannot find Cabernet Sauvignon grapes, then you can use some other similar red wine grape. The first day you will be processing the grapes, whether you bought or picked them.

1. When you get the grapes home you will want to rinse and clean them thoroughly. Remove bad grapes and debris. If you allow the grapes to sit for a couple hours, most insects will make their way to the top of the grapes, which will make it easier to dispose of them.

2. Remove all the stems by hand and discard them. You should not allow any stems into your wine as they may impart a bitter taste.

3. You will need to crush the grapes. Do not use a food processor, as the seeds can impart bitter and undesirable flavors. You could crush the grapes by hand if it is a small batch or place in a small fruit press. If you do use a press, do not press them all the way. You just want to break the skins. You can also choose to crush the grapes like your ancestors did, by stomping them. Be sure to sanitize your feet well. You will want to catch the event on film. You can place the grapes in a plastic fermentation bucket and then jump in with your bare sanitized feet. The goal is to break the skins to allow the juice to seep out.

4. After you have crushed the grapes and the juice has begun to flow you may want to perform an acid and sugar test. This is not totally

necessary to make wine. I only include it here as a place marker for when you perform these types of tests. These readings are important if you want to have complete control over the final results. These tests will determine sugar and acid levels; they will not guarantee you will have an award-winning wine. In order to perform these tests you will need to extract some of the juice from the fermenter. Use the results to decide whether you will need to add more sugar or possibly dilute the mixture.

5. You can raise the sugar level by adding small amounts of sugar (by the cup) or you can use grape juice concentrate. You will want to do this slowly and check the readings before adding any more sugar or juice. Remember you can always add more but once the sugar or juice is mixed in you cannot take it away. You will want to determine ahead of time whether you want a sweet wine or a dry wine. You will want to also determine whether you want a high alcohol wine or low. Sugar controls how sweet and what the potential alcohol level will be. Once you have determined what kind of wine you want to create, you will want to choose the right yeast. Most wine yeast can withstand an alcohol content of 12 to 14 percent alcohol. If you want sweeter wine you will want to add more sugar than the yeast can convert to alcohol. For a drier wine you will want to have just enough sugar. If you want a higher alcohol content then you will want to raise the specific gravity and choose a higher alcohol-tolerant yeast strain.

6. Adjusting the acid level will affect the mouth feel of a wine. Too little acid will make it have a soft and dilute mouth feel, whereas too much acid can negatively affect the yeast and create too tart a wine. Your target acid should be: 0.6 to 0.7 percent in red wines and 0.7 to 0.8 percent in whites.

7. Once you have determined your wine is ready for fermentation, you will want to kill off any wild yeasts or bacteria that can negatively affect your wine by turning it into vinegar, stopping fermentation, or ruining the taste of your finished product. The simplest way to sterilize your wine must is to add sulfites. As I have mentioned in this book, I do not recommend over-sulfiting your wine. Add an average of 1/2 teaspoon of metabisulphite for every 5 to 6 gallons of wine. I use campden tablets, which are measures of compressed sulfite powder. If you use campden tablets, crush them by hand or use the back of a spoon against a tabletop.

8. The largest difference of a red wine is that you will be shortly fermenting the wine with the skins still present. You will want this fermentation to be slow, so you will want to cool the must. A simple way to cool the must is to place sealable plastic bags filled with frozen water in the must. Before placing the bags in the must, make sure you have sanitized them. You do not have to do this, but you should place the must in a dark, cool place. The must will need to rest 24 hours in order for the sulphite to "gas off."

9. After 24 hours you will pitch (add) your yeast into the must. You will use one packet for up to 6 gallons of wine.

Days 2 to 12:

1. You are ready to move onto the maceration stage of red winemaking. This is also referred to as fermenting on the skins. You want this part of the fermentation process to go slowly. You will want to replace your ice bags if you are using them. You will see the term "punch down the cap." The skins will often float to the top of the vessel and form a hard crust. You will want to push these skins back into the must to get the most color and tannins possible for a color-

ful, full-bodied red wine. You can punch down the cap by hand or use a paddle or spoon. Whatever you decide to use, make sure you sanitize your hands and equipment.

2. The length of time the wine macerates is totally up to the individual. The longer you leave them, the more tannins are released. Tannins give a certain mouth feel and can feel slightly astringent on the tongue. You do not want too many tannins or it will be unpalatable. Too little tannins and the wine will be considered weak or not very complex. There is a window for the length as far as the wine color is concerned. For up to seven days the wine will get a darker shade of red. After seven days the color will begin to get lighter. The wine will continue to lighten but tannins will continue to be released.

3. If you want the best-tasting wine possible, do not press the skins when you remove them. The juice in your fermenter will create the highest quality wine. The juice you press from the grapes will be weaker and pales in comparison. You could decide to create two different wines. The wine created from pressing the grapes is referred to as second-run wine. Unless you have a lot of juice from the first run you may want to press all the juice from the grapes and mix it with the first-run juice. The result will not be bad wine, it is juice not as complex as a first-run wine without the grapes pressed.

4. You may want to own a small press to press the grape skins. You can get away with making a homemade press at home, but the mess you will save yourself is worth the small investment. Add the crushed grapes to your press and press the juice either into your primary vessel or in a second vessel if you are making second-run wine. Make sure everything is sanitized before you begin pressing.

Do not ratchet the press all the way down because you could crush the seeds, which can give a bitter taste to your wine. You can dry out the grape skins and use them as fire kindling or you can compost them in your garden.

5. Make sure you do not have too much headroom in your vessel. You can add more wine or grape juice of the same variety to make up the difference. Unless noted in the recipe, do not dilute it with water or this can dilute the taste of your wine. If you have some extra juice, seal it in jugs, without adding yeast to top off your wine during racking.

Days 40 to 60

1. The wine should begin to slow fermentation and be completed between 40 and 60 days from the time you started the wine. This includes primary and secondary or malolactic fermentation. During this period of time it is recommended that once primary fermentation begins to slow down you rack the wine into a carboy to begin secondary fermentation. You will know it is stopping by the how rapidly the bubbling is in the fermentation lock. Secondary formation mellows the wine and makes it smoother to drink. This is the time when different unwanted chemicals are moved by the yeast such as diacetyl, acetylaldehyde, and some sulphur compounds. During secondary fermentation you will begin to see a sediment form. This is called trub (pronounced "troob") and is made up of dead yeasts and other proteins. You will begin to see the wine become clearer and easier to see through. It is at this time that you can add clarifiers to draw even more proteins that are suspended in the wine to the bottom of the carboy. Malolactic fermentation also refers to the process of removing malic acid. This is accomplished

when the lactic acid bacteria consume the malic acid for energy. This process can occur naturally in wines or you may chose to add lactic acid bacteria during secondary fermentation.

2. Once fermentation has completely ceased you may choose to bottle or age the wine. You will know that fermentation has ceased by consistent hydrometer readings. In the recipes in this book you will see FG at the top. This is the final gravity and gives you an idea of what you are looking for as a final specific gravity reading. You choose to add stabilizers like campden tablets to ensure the wine will not begin fermentation in the bottle or while aging.

Aging

1. After the readings on the hydrometer are stable you may choose to skip to bottling. However, aging a wine will make a smoother, more mellow and complex flavor. It does take some willpower. Many home winemakers want to try to drink a wine as quickly as possible. If you can just wait a little, the taste will only improve. You do want to make sure you have racked the wine off the sediment or "lees" because they can begin to decay in a process called autolysis, which will alter the flavor of your wine. Even during the aging period you may occasionally rack the wine into another carboy if you see sediment forming.

2. You may choose to age your wine in an oak barrel. Some people do not like the taste of oak, while others will swear by it. It is purely a matter of taste and preference. Remember, this is your wine and you get to decide how it will turn out. You do have the option of adding oak chips to the carboy instead of barrel-aging your wine. I have used this low-cost alternative with great success.

3. During the process of aging wine, some evaporation occurs. This is completely natural; however, it creates headspace. This can allow bad bacteria to have a place to form, which can ruin your wine. You can add just a few cups of a similar wine without affecting the taste of the wine you are aging. It is better to use wine than grape juice because the sugars in raw juice can cause fermentation to reoccur.

4. Make sure you are aging your wine in a dark, cold environment. Not everyone can have their own private cave to age their wine in. Try to create the effect of a cave by placing your wine in a basement or even in a crawl space under your home. If you seal your vessel well you should not have to worry about any insects getting into your wine. As long as your wine is cold and stable you can seal a vessel without fear of it exploding.

5. You may want to check your wine for taste and character as it ages. Try to keep this to a minimum because you risk contamination every time you unseal a vessel. If you take wine out you should fill it up to reduce headspace.

6. At the six-month mark you may want to consider racking the wine, especially if any sediment has formed. This is a good time to test and taste your wine.

7. If your wine smells bad or is not clearing, you may want to check the troubleshooting chapter at the end of this book. There is the possibility that a wine will go bad. Most of the time a wine goes bad because of bad sanitation procedures. Being clean and sanitizing will reduce the risk of contaminated wine significantly.

8. You may decide to filter your wine before bottling. This is totally unnecessary, especially since the scale of winemaking most home-

winemakers create is small. Remember that filtering can remove the good with the bad; your wine could become pale and flat-tasting.

9. Make sure there are no changes in your hydrometer readings. Once you are sure your wine is ready, it is time to bottle your wine. Rack the wine off lees and into a primary fermenter bucket. This is now your bottling bucket. Attach a tube from the bottom spigot with a bottle filler at the end of the tubing. Make sure there is no fermentation lock on the lid. Filling the bottle will create a vacuum that can pull the water right from the fermentation lock into your wine. Make sure you have plenty of sanitized bottles ready to be filled. Once you fill them, cork them immediately. The less time your wine is exposed to the air the better. Oxygen can begin to break down and oxidize your wine. This can lead to a metallic, flat taste that can only be cured by pouring perfectly good wine down the drain.

10. After bottling, be sure to allow the wine to settle a few weeks before opening.

More Tips on Aging

Some people have questions about how long they should age their wine. Here are some suggestions based upon the type of wine you are aging. Keep in mind that if you are using barrels, you can use a barrel that you aged white wine in for either a white or red wine. If you age red wine in a barrel, you can only use it for red wines from then on.

1. If you are allowing full-bodied red wines to age, they should be allowed to mature for at least a year. If you have the patience, allow them to mature for two to three years. Unless you have an iron will and great patience, you probably will not wait that long.

2. If you are creating light red and rose wines then you should them to mature six months to a full year before drinking.

3. If you are aging a full-flavored white wine try to age them for a minimum of six months; a year is better.

4. If you decide to age a light, fruity white wine you should age it for at least three months, but six months is even better.

White Wines

There is not much difference between making a white wine and red wine. The greatest difference in the process occurs in the beginning. Instead of fermenting on the skins, the skins are pressed just after they are crushed. The skins never touch the fermenting must. This gives white wine a different character because it contains less tannin and it does not have the red ruby color. Other than that the process is exactly the same.

Here is a list of common white wine varietals:

- Albariño / Alvarinho
- Chardonnay
- Chenin Blanc
- Gewürztraminer
- Muscat
- Pinot Blanc
- Pinot Gris/Pinot Grigio
- Riesling
- Sauvignon Blanc
- Émillon
- Viognier

You can try some of these varietals on your own to get some practice making wine. The bulk of this book is dedicated to wild wines that could contain any plant that has some level of residual sugar.

Blending Wines

The United States is one of the only countries that names wines according to their varietal, such as chardonnay or Merlot. In Europe wines are named after the regions they come from, such as Chianti or Boudreaux. Many times blended wines are given the names of these regions according to the types of wines they usually produce. For instance Chianti is made from grapes in the Chianti region in Italy. It is based upon a certain recipe for blending wine in that region.

The idea behind blending wines is that the whole is greater than the sum of its parts. There are some varietals that blend together well to create a better wine then the three wines would be if they stood alone.

I created Chianti wine that won a gold medal at an international wine competition. The recipe consisted of 70 percent Sangiovese, 15 percent Canaiolo, and 15 percent Malvasia Bianca. There are two ways in which this could be created.

The first way is to blend the juices in the proportions mentioned and ferment them together as one wine. The other way is to create three different wines and then blend them together.

The first method of juice blending is easier if you have the proportions already worked out through someone else's recipe or through experience creating the blended wine in the past.

The second method gives you more control over the final blend. You would take small amounts of the three wines and mix them together in different proportions. Write down the results with the exact proportions you used.

I recommend you experiment using the second method. If you try to blend at the beginning of fermentation you could ruin the whole batch. Some blends do not turn out palatable.

I recommend trying up to five combinations at a time (often referred to as a flight). Your palate can not truly discern the taste of the wine if you try a larger flight. The tannins and alcohol can overwork your tongue and taste buds. If you find a blend you like, put it aside overnight. The next day try the combination again and see if you still like the blend. Once you have found a blend you like, then you can mix the wines in the exact same proportions you did when mixing small amounts.

Do not mix wines before you have tried them out in small proportions. You will work hard to create wines and working too quickly can ruin it all.

Another type of blending that is used by wineries worldwide is mixing different wines from different regions. The wines can be the same varietal but have slightly different imperfections caused by soil, water or climate. By mixing different wines these slight imperfections can be erased.

In order for wineries to produce consistent-tasting wine year after year, they often use this type of blending. They will often reserve wine from different vintages and use it to blend with wine to bring it closer to the standard wine they produce year after year.

CASE STUDY: GEORGE M. WALKER

cpowalker@aol.com
909-466-7097
Home winemaker and winery owner

I have been a home winemaker since 1994. It is a very en-
joyable and satisfying hobby. Friends and family love to receive the wine as gifts, and most like to participate in the
annual harvest, crush, and bottling events that I have held
over the years. I've come to further enjoy it because I have refined my processes, the wine has improved, and I have won a number of national awards for
both my wines and for my custom labels. Winemaking is truly a form of art that
requires a certain amount of know-how, experience, commitment, and passion.
My hobby turned into a "Co-operative" of family and friends a few years ago.
We now have 14 families doing the work while I make the wine. Check out our
Web site at: **www.cucamongacoop.org** and **www.walkerfamilyvintners.com**.

When I was in seventh grade back in my home state of Indiana, I did a science
project making wine from Welch's® grape juice. It was god-awful stuff, but I
wouldn't have known the difference anyway since I wasn't a wine-lover back
then! I think my dad liked it, though, because it slowly disappeared over time.
I later learned to appreciate wine when I was in college and was introduced to
a nice Chateau Neuf Du Pape at a nice dinner with my fraternity advisor. Years
later, my wife and I moved to a new home in Indianapolis. As luck would have it, a
home wine- and beer-making shop was located just down the street and around
the corner. Having the urge to start a hobby, I visited the store and bought a basic
home winemaker start kit with all the essentials for making a five-gallon batch of
wine from a kit. As they say, "the rest is history." The full, historical account can
be found at my Web site.

I have many favorite wines, but I suppose the wine that I drink the most is Zinfandel (not to be confused with White Zinfandel). Old Vines Zinfandel grows
here in our Cucamonga Appellation of Southern California, so I guess I enjoy
drinking from the area's winemaking heritage. A good Zinfandel is a wonderful thing. However, Zinfandels from different climates have different tastes and
character. I guess I enjoy our locally grown and vinted Zinfandel the most. (Au-
thor's note — "vinted" means "creating a wine from."

While living in Indiana, there was a great winery that made primarily fruit wines
and some wines from cold-hardy grape varietals (such as Concord and Catawa-
ba). Of those, I particularly loved their blackberry wine.

CASE STUDY: GEORGE M. WALKER

I have won many awards for my wines. I didn't start entering my wines into competitions until 2004. I guess I just became aware of such competitions from looking on the Internet. Since 2004, I have won 30 awards for 20 of my wines in various competitions around the nation. They can be viewed on my Web site.

I recommend other amateur winemakers also compete in competitions. Besides your own palate and your friends' feedback (hopefully objective), a competition can give you great objective and professional feedback as most of them provide the home winemakers with the judges' tasting notes. Some judges also give specific, helpful feedback to the entrant. Here are a few competitions: **www.cellarmastersla.com**; Orange County, California Fair; Indiana State Fair; and WineMaker Magazine Annual Competition. Just do an online search on keywords such as "amateur winemaking competition" or "home winemaking competition." I've only been able to personally observe a few competitions, and I was very nervous and excited.

Many wineries in the upper Midwest make wines from fruit and other sources, such as honey and dandelions. Indiana wineries also do this. You can get all the names, addresses, and Web sites from **www.indianawines.org/wineries/**.

Beginner wine kits are pretty standard at the winemaking supply stores. Some starter kits have just the very basics, while other kits are "deluxe" and have better quality or additional equipment. Here are the basics from memory: Large bucket for primary fermentation; plastic stirring spoon; hydrometer for measuring specific gravity, and calculating alcohol; grape or fruit concentrate; wine yeast; potassium metabisulphite powder; liquid oak essence or other oak alternative like chips or cubes; wine clarifier; five- or six-gallon carboy for secondary fermentation and clarification; racking tube and hose; airlock; corks; bottles; and good corker (table top or floor stand models). Some intermediate and advanced equipment a winemaker should consider is a Sulphite tester, Acid tester, pH meter, small barrel(s), and a racking pump (hand or electric).

I still like red wine with red meat and white wine with white meat, but I'll drink any wine with any pairing!

CHAPTER 3

Other Fruit Wines

CASE STUDY: PABLO SOLOMON

IInternational artist and sculptor
www.pablosolomon.com

When I was a kid I lived in one of the poorest neighborhoods in Houston. It was literally across the street from a railroad yard and in the shadows of downtown skyscrapers. Who would expect a winemaker in that setting? But there was one. Around the corner was an old house — most in our neighborhood were built in the 1880s. It stood out because the yard was always neat and the old lady who owned it swept her sidewalk and curb every day. She also had magnificent peach and plum trees growing in her backyard and she guarded them with ferocity. One day my mother and I were walking to the store. In those days we went every day to get fresh produce. The old lady was out in her yard and commented to my mother that she thought I was a good-looking little boy in my straw hat. They started talking and she invited us into her house. It was mind bending. She had several rooms filled from floor to ceiling with wine bottles. You only had a small path through each room. She had thousands of bottles of wine. And she had made them all herself from the peach and plum fruit she grew. She had a few oak casks. I was too young to ask many questions, but I always remembered her. She gave my mother a bottle of wine and my mom and dad had it with their supper. They said it was good. Some of the kids called her a "bruja" (witch), but I thought she was a magical person since she could make wine in such a poor setting.

Because you have learned the basics, in this chapter you will learn how to make wild wines. These are wines that shake up and change the sugar sources and yeast types. If you have the chance you can experiment on your own using different water. You can have friends save water from their springs or municipal supply. This section will discuss different kinds of fruits and how they can be made into a wine. Some of these will be solely fruits and some will be blends of fruit and grape or combination of fruits.

Make sure you pick fruits and vegetables when they are fresh and in season. Many of the fruits you can buy year round at the grocery store may lack flavor and even essential sugars. Buy what is in season. It is not the best idea to start a watermelon wine in the dead of winter.

You can go to farmer's markets, as they will always have fruits and vegetables that are fresh and in season. Winemaking is about planning ahead. You need to think now what you want to drink next year.

If you just cannot wait to make that raspberry wine, you do have the option to buy berries frozen. This is a good option because they are often flash frozen just after they are picked. They retain sugars, flavor, and color. Make sure you defrost the fruit before dumping it into a fermenter. The freezing cold fruit can slow done or even stunt fermentation.

Frozen fruit has another advantage. When the juices crystallize in the fruit as it freezes, the crystals are often jagged. These crystals break the cell walls in the fruit, or even vegetable. This allows juice to flow freely when it is defrosted because it is not trapped inside the fruit. Even if you buy fresh fruit, you may want to freeze it for a few days before using it in a wine.

Berry Wines

Berries are actually produced by the single ovary of a plant. The entire wall of the ovary ripens and can be eaten. The seeds of the berry are usually embedded in the flesh of the fruit. There are many types of fruits that are called berries, but are not technically berries at all — such as blueberries, cranberries, raspberries, and strawberries. I have included these types of false berries in this section on berry wines. Most berries are great to use for wine because they usually contain a lot of sugar and are full of flavor.

Frankenberry Wine

Yield 1 gallon/3.8 L

OG = 1.09 FG = 1.014 ABV = 10%

Ingredients:

- 4 lbs boysenberries (fresh or frozen)
- 2 ¼ lb granulated sugar
- ½ tsp pectic enzyme
- ½ tsp acid blend
- 1 Campden tablet
- Water
- 1 packet wine yeast
- 1 tsp yeast nutrient
- 1-gallon carboy
- Standard winemaking equipment

Instructions:

1. Wash the boysenberries thoroughly. You can do this using a colander.

2. Use your hands to crush berries in a bowl. Place them in a nylon bag or cheesecloth.

3. Transfer the berry bag to your fermentation bucket. Add a campden tablet.

4. Pour a gallon of boiling water over fruit bag. Allow to sit for 48 hours.

5. Gently squeeze the bag and remove. Add sugar and acidic blend. Stir well to make sure it is completely dissolved. Add pectic enzyme, cover well, and allow it to sit for 24 hours.

6. Add the yeast and nutrient.

7. Cover, and set aside five to six days, stirring daily.

8. Rack into carboy and attach airlock.

9. Allow the wine to sit for three months in a cool, dark place.

10. Rack the wine and allow it to sit for another two months.

11. Rack it again and bottle.

12. Give it one year to mature.

Goosey Berry

Yield 5 gallons/19 L

OG = 1.088 FG = 1.014 ABV = 10%

Ingredients:

- 13 lbs gooseberries
- 11 lbs granulated sugar
- ½ tsp pectic enzyme
- Water
- Packet of champagne yeast

- Standard winemaking equipment
- Cheesecloth or nylon bag
- ½ tsp of tannin
- 1 tbsp yeast energizer

Instructions:

1. Wash the gooseberries thoroughly. You can do this using a colander.

2. Use your hands to crush berries in a bowl. Place them in a nylon bag or cheesecloth. Pour juice created by crushing the berries into the fermenter.

3. Transfer the berry bag to your fermentation bucket.

4. Pour a gallon of boiling water over fruit bag. Allow to sit for 48 hours.

5. Gently squeeze the bag and remove. Add sugar and stir well to make sure it is completely dissolved. Add pectic enzyme, cover well, and allow it to sit for 24 hours.

6. Add the yeast, energizer, and tannin.

7. Cover, and set aside five to six days, stirring daily.

8. Pour into carboy and attach airlock.

9. Allow the wine to sit for three months in a cool, dark place.

10. Rack the wine and allow it to sit for another two months.

11. Rack it again and bottle.

12. Give it one year to mature.

All Around the Mulberry Bush

Yield 1 gallon/3.8 L

OG = 1.09 FG = 1.014 ABV = 10%

Ingredients:

- 6 cups mulberries, fresh (Make sure they are not overripe or spoiled)
- 1 tsp yeast nutrient
- 5 cups granulated sugar
- 3 campden tablets
- 1 packet wine yeast
- ½ tsp pectic enzyme
- Water
- Standard winemaking equipment
- Nylon Bag/Cheesecloth
- 1-gallon carboy
- 1 tbsp yeast energizer

Instructions:

1. Wash the mulberries thoroughly. You can do this using a colander.

2. Use your hands to crush berries in a bowl. Place them in a nylon bag or cheesecloth. Transfer the berry bag to your fermentation bucket. Pour juice produced in bowl into the fermentation bucket.

3. Pour a gallon of boiling water over fruit bag. Allow to sit for 48 hours.

4. Gently squeeze the bag and remove. Add sugar and stir well to make sure it is completely dissolved. Add pectic enzyme, cover well, and allow it to sit for 24 hours.

5. Add yeast, energizer, nutrient and tannin.

6. Cover and set aside for five to six days, stirring daily.

7. Pour into carboy and attach airlock.

8. Allow the wine to sit for three months in a cool, dark place.

9. Rack the wine, add campden tablets and allow it to sit for another two months.

10. Rack it again and bottle.

11. Give it a year to mature.

Around the Mulberry Bush Again

Yield 1 gallon/3.8 L

OG = 1.09 FG = 1.014 ABV = 10%

Ingredients:

- 20 cups fresh mulberries
- 1 tsp yeast nutrient
- Standard winemaking equipment

- 4 ½ cups granulated sugar
- 3 campden tablets
- 1 packet wine yeast
- Water
- ½ tsp pectic enzyme
- 1-gallon carboy

Instructions:

1. Wash the mulberries thoroughly. You can do this using a colander.

2. Place berries in bag/cloth and crush in the primary fermenter. Add sugar, water, crushed campden tablet, pectic enzyme, and nutrients. Stir the mixture in order to dissolve sugar. Let sit 24 hours.

3. Make sure your specific gravity is between 1.090 and 1.095. Pitch yeast and stir. Keep stirring daily for five or six days until the specific gravity is 1.040. Remove bag and gently squeeze out juice. Rack into carboy and attach an airlock.

4. If you wish for your wine to be dry then you should allow it to mature for three weeks, rack the wine, and let it mature for another four weeks. When the wine is clear and no longer needs racking, it is ready to bottle.

5. For a sweeter wine, mature wine for three weeks, then rack into another vessel. Dissolve ½ cup sugar in 1 cup wine and pour the sweetened wine back into the fermentation vessel. Repeat every six weeks or when at least two hydrometer readings are stable. Rack every month until the wine is clear, then bottle.

6. Allow your wine to mature for two years.

Old Man Wine

Yield 1 gallon/3.8 L

OG = 1.09 FG = 1.014 ABV = 10%

Ingredients:

- 4 ½ cups elderberries
- Water
- 1 lemon, juice only
- 5 ¾ cups sugar
- 1 campden tablet
- 1 tsp yeast nutrients
- 1 tsp pectic enzyme
- 1 packet wine yeast
- Standard winemaking equipment
- 1 gallon carboy
- Nylon cloth/cheesecloth

Instructions:

1. Wash berries and remove stalks. Place berries in cloth and crush over fermenter and place bag in bottom. Crush campden tablets into primary fermenter. Stir in pectic enzyme and lemon juice. Let sit for 24 hours.

2. Add a quart of water and pitch yeast. Stir daily for three days. Punch down the fruit if necessary. Punching the fruit means that you are using a stick or your sterilized hands and physically pushing the fruit back into the wine must.

3. On the fourth day strain out the fruit and add the sugar and nutrients. Rack into carboy and attach airlock.

4. For a dry wine, rack in three weeks, and again in four weeks. Keep racking every month until wine is clear in the bottle.

5. For a sweeter tasting wine, mature for three weeks, then rack into another vessel. Dissolve ½-cup sugar in 1 cup wine and pour the

sweetened wine back into the fermentation vessel. Add crushed campden tablet. Repeat every six weeks or when at least two hydrometer readings are stable. Rack the wine every month until the wine is clear, then bottle.

6. Mature wine for one year from the date you started the process.

Old Woman Wine

Yield 1 gallon/3.8 L

OG = 1.09 FG = 1.014 ABV = 10%

Ingredients:

- 4 ½ cups elderberries
- 12 cups water
- 10 cups raisins
- 3 campden tablets
- 1 tsp pectic enzyme
- 1 tsp yeast nutrients
- 1 packet wine yeast
- Standard winemaking equipment
- 1 gallon carboy
- Nylon bag/cheesecloth

Instructions:

1. Chop raisins. Put into bag and in primary fermenter with 10 cups cold water. Crush campden tablets into fermenter. Let sit for 24 hours.

2. Add yeast and nutrients. Stir each day for two weeks.

3. After two weeks, wash elderberries thoroughly and remove the stems. Place berries in a non-metal container in the oven at 250 F for 15 minutes or until juice runs. Remove raisin bag. Place berries in cloth and press juice into the fermenter.

4. Add pectic enzyme. Stir.

5. Rack into carboy and attach airlock.

6. If you wish for your wine to be dry then you should allow it to mature for three weeks, rack the wine and then allow it to mature for another four weeks. When the wine is clear and no longer needs racking, then it is ready to bottle.

7. For a sweeter tasting wine, mature for three weeks, then rack into another vessel. Dissolve ½ cup sugar in 1 cup wine and pour the sweetened wine back into the fermentation vessel. You may consider adding another campden tablet. Repeat every six weeks or when at least two hydrometer readings are stable. Rack the wine every month until the wine is clear, then bottle.

8. Mature wine a year from the date you started the process.

Sour Kiss

Yield 5 gallons/19 L

OG = 1.088 FG = 1.014 ABV = 10%

Ingredients:

- 15 lbs persimmons
- 10 ½ lbs granulated sugar
- 3/4 tsp pectic enzyme
- Water
- Packet of champagne yeast
- Standard winemaking equipment
- Cheesecloth or nylon bag
- 1 tbsp yeast energizer
- ½ tsp wine tannin
- 3 tbsp of acid blend

Instructions:

1. Wash persimmons thoroughly in colander.

2. Crush persimmons by hand in a bowl and place them in a nylon bag or cheesecloth.

3. Transfer the berry bag to your fermentation bucket.

4. Pour a gallon of boiling water over fruit bag. Allow to sit for 48 hours.

5. Gently squeeze the bag and remove. Add sugar and stir well to make sure it is completely dissolved. Add pectic enzyme, add water to 5-gallon level, cover well, and allow it to sit for 24 hours.

6. Add yeast, energizer, and tannin; cover, and set aside five to six days, stirring daily.

7. Pour into carboy and attach airlock.

8. Allow the wine to sit for three months in a cool dark place.

9. Rack the wine and then allow it to sit for another two months.

10. Rack your wine again and bottle.

11. Allow a year to mature.

Blueberry Wine

Yield 1 gallon/3.8 L

OG = 1.09 FG = 1.014 ABV = 10%

Ingredients:

- 4 to 5 cups blueberries
- 5 cups granulated sugar
- 2 tsp acid blend
- ½ tsp pectic enzyme
- 1 tsp nutrients
- 2 campden tablets
- 1 packet wine yeast
- Water
- Standard winemaking equipment
- 1-gallon carboy
- Nylon bag/cheesecloth

Instructions:

1. Place fruit into cheesecloth/bag. Place in primary fermenter and crush the fruit. Transfer the berry bag to your fermentation bucket.

2. Pour a gallon of boiling water over fruit bag. Add campden tablet. Allow to sit for 48 hours.

3. Gently squeeze the bag and remove. Add sugar and stir well to make sure it is completely dissolved. Add pectic enzyme, cover well, and allow it to sit for 24 hours.

4. Add yeast, nutrients, and tannin; cover, and set aside five to six days, stirring daily.

5. Pour into carboy and attach airlock.

6. For a drier tasting wine the wine should mature for at least three weeks after which the wine should be racked and allowed to mature four more weeks. The wine should be clear and the hydrometer readings stable before it is bottled.

7. For a sweeter tasting wine, mature for three weeks, then rack into another vessel. Dissolve ½ cup sugar in 1 cup wine and pour the sweetened wine back into the fermentation vessel. Repeat every six weeks or when at least two hydrometer readings are stable. Rack the wine every month until the wine is clear, then bottle.

8. Mature wine a year from the date it was started.

To create a fuller flavored wine you can add 1 cup red grape juice at the time of bottling. Make sure you add another campden tablet to stabilize wine.

Blueberry Port

Yield 1 gallon/3.8 L

OG = 1.09 FG = .990 ABV = 14%

Ingredients:

- 6 lbs (12 cups) blueberries
- ½ cup dry malt
- 4 cups granulated sugar
- ½ tsp acid blend
- ½ tsp pectic enzyme
- 1 tsp yeast nutrient
- 2 campden tablets
- 1 package sherry or port yeast
- Water
- Standard winemaking equipment
- 1-gallon carboy

Instructions:

1. Place fruit into cheesecloth/bag. Place in primary fermenter and crush the fruit. Transfer the berry bag to your fermentation bucket.

2. Pour a gallon of boiling water over fruit bag. Add campden tablet. Allow to sit for 48 hours.

3. Gently squeeze the bag and remove. Add sugar and stir well to make sure it is completely dissolved. Add pectic enzyme, cover well, and allow it to sit for 24 hours.

4. Add yeast, nutrients, and tannin; cover, and set aside five to six days, stirring daily.

5. Pour into carboy and attach airlock.

6. For a drier tasting wine, the wine should mature for at least three weeks after which the wine should be racked and allowed to mature four more weeks. The wine should be clear and the hydrometer readings stable before it is bottled.

7. For a sweeter tasting wine, mature for three weeks, then rack into another vessel. Dissolve ½ cup sugar in 1 cup wine and pour the sweetened wine back into the fermentation vessel. Repeat every six weeks or when at least two hydrometer readings are stable. Rack the wine every month until the wine is clear, then bottle.

8. Allow port wine to mature for at least a year and half from when you started creating the port.

Red and Blue

Yield 5 gallons/19 L

OG= 1.105 FG= 0.995 ABV= 11%

Ingredients:

- 12 lbs blueberries
- 1 quart red wine juice concentrate
- 9 lbs cane sugar
- 1 tsp acid blend
- 2 tsp yeast nutrient
- 2 tsp pectic enzyme
- 1 tsp tannin
- 8 campden tablets
- Water

- 1 packet of Montpellier wine yeast
- Standard winemaking equipment
- Nylon bag/cheesecloth

Instructions:

1. Place blueberries in nylon bag and crush. If you have a fruit press you may also use this. Place the blueberries in the cheesecloth and place in the primary fermenter.

2. Add grape juice, 6 qt of hot water, acid blend, and sugar to the blueberries.

3. Stir the mixture until the sugar is dissolved.

4. Add yeast nutrient, pectic enzyme, tannin, campden tablets, and enough cold water to bring the level to five gallons. Check specific gravity and adjust if necessary.

5. Once the temperature is down to 75 degrees F, pitch the yeast.

6. Cover fermenter and add fermentation look. Stir twice a day until SG is 1.020.

7. Squeeze cheesecloth and remove from fermenter. Rack into carboy.

8. Place in a cooler location (65 degrees F or less) for 10 days or when SG reaches 1.000.

9. Rack must into a fermentation unit and top with water to 5-gallon level. Allow to settle for three weeks or when SG is 0.995. Rack into bottling bucket and bottle.

10. Allow wine to mature for nine to 12 months before drinking.

Rowanberry, or dogberries, can cause indigestion if they are eaten raw. Heating or freezing the berries removes this property from the berries.

Dog Berry Wine

Yield 1 gallon/3.8 L

OG = 1.09 FG = 1.014 ABV = 10%

Ingredients:

- 16 cups rowanberries, picked after first frost
- 8 cups brown sugar
- 1 tsp yeast nutrient
- 1 tsp acid blend
- 1 campden tablet
- 1 tea bag *

- 1 packet wine yeast
- Water
- Standard winemaking equipment
- 1-gallon carboy
- Nylon bag/cheesecloth

Instructions:

1. Remove the stems off the berries and wash them. Place berries in bag/cloth and crush; then place in primary fermenter. Add tea bag to boiling water and boil for five minutes. Add the tea to the fermenter. Let sit 24 hours.

2. Add nutrients, sugar, acid blend, and crushed campden tablet. Stir vigorously in order to dissolve sugar. The SG should be between 1.090 and 1.095. Pitch yeast and stir. Stir the wine must for three to five days, until specific gravity reading is 1.040.

3. Remove bag and squeeze out as much juice as you can from the fruit. Rack into carboy and attach airlock.

4. If you wish for your wine to be dry then you should allow it to mature for three weeks, rack the wine, and then allow it to mature for another four weeks. When the wine is clear and no longer needs racking, then it is ready to bottle.

5. For a sweeter tasting wine, mature for three weeks, then rack into another vessel. Dissolve ½ cup sugar in 1 cup wine and pour the sweetened wine back into the fermentation vessel. Repeat every six weeks or when at least two hydrometer readings are stable. Rack the wine every month until the wine is clear, then bottle.

6. For the best results, allow the wine to mature for are least one year from the date it was started before you drink it.

You can replace tea bag with 1/8 tsp of tannin.

Giving it the Raspberry

Yield 5 gallons/19 L

OG = 1.088 FG = 1.014 ABV = 10%

Ingredients:

- 15 lbs raspberries
- 10 ½ lbs granulated sugar
- ¾ tsp pectic enzyme
- Water
- Packet of ICV D47
- Standard winemaking equipment
- Cheesecloth or nylon bag
- 2 tbsp yeast nutrient
- 2 ½ tbsp acid blend

Instructions:

1. Wash berries well. You can use a colander.

2. Crush berries in a bowl and place them in a nylon bag or cheesecloth.

3. Place bag to into fermentation bucket.

4. Pour a gallon of boiling water over fruit bag. Allow to sit for 48 hours.

5. Gently squeeze the bag and remove. Add sugar and stir well to make sure it is completely dissolved. Add pectic enzyme, add water to 5-gallon level, cover well, and set aside for 24 hours.

6. Add yeast, nutrient, acid blend; cover, and set aside five to six days, stirring daily.

7. Pour into carboy. Fit airlock.

8. Place in cool (60-65 degrees F) dark place for three months.

9. Rack to a carboy; allow it to mature for another two months.

10. Rack the clear wine and bottle.

11. Allow wine to mature a year.

Black Eye Wine

Yield 1 gallon/3.8 L

OG = 1.088 FG = 1.014 ABV = 10%

Ingredients:

- 6 lbs blackberries
- 2 ½ lbs granulated sugar
- ½ tsp pectic enzyme
- 7 pints water
- ¼ tsp wine yeast

- Primary fermentation vessel
- Cheesecloth or nylon bag
- 1-gallon carboy
- 1 tsp yeast nutrient
- Standard winemaking equipment

Instructions:

1. Wash berries thoroughly in colander.

2. Crush berries in a bowl and place them in a nylon bag or cheesecloth.

3. Transfer bag to primary fermentation vessel.

4. Pour 7 pints of boiling water over fruit bag. Allow to sit for 48 hours.

5. Gently squeeze the bag and remove. Add sugar and stir well to make sure it is completely dissolved. Stir in pectic enzyme and allow it to sit for 24 hours.

6. Pitch yeast and nutrient. Stir every day for five to six days.

7. Pour into carboy. Attach airlock.

8. Place wine in a cool, dark place for three months.

9. Rack and allow it to sit for another two months.

10. Rack again and bottle.

11. Allow a year to mature.

Pure Black Gold

This recipe contains only fruit and no added water

Yield 1 gallon/3.8 L

OG = 1.09 FG = 1.014 ABV = 10%

Ingredients:

- 15 lbs fresh blackberries (Do not use over-ripe berries)
- 4 ½ cups granulated sugar
- 1 tsp yeast nutrient
- 2 campden tablets
- ½ tsp pectic enzyme
- 1 packet wine yeast
- Standard winemaking equipment
- 1-gallon carboy

Instructions:

1. Crush the berries in bottom of primary fermenter.

2. Add sugar, pectic enzyme, and crushed campden tablets. Stir well to dissolve sugar.

3. Create a yeast starter by adding yeast to ½ cup to 1 cup water or orange juice, yeast nutrient and 1 tsp of sugar. Cover tightly and shake well. Allow to sit 24 hours.

4. Pitch yeast starter to berries. Stir well. Cover loosely and stir several times per day for four days. Break the hard crust that will form on top of berries daily.

5. Squeeze out as much juice as you can from the fruit and rack wine must into a carboy and attach airlock.

6. For a drier tasting wine the wine should mature for at least three weeks after which the wine should be racked and allowed to mature

four more weeks. The wine should be clear and the hydrometer readings stable before it is bottled.

7. For a sweeter tasting wine, mature wine for three weeks, then rack into another vessel. Dissolve ½ cup sugar in 1 cup wine and pour the sweetened wine back into the fermentation vessel. Repeat until at least two hydrometer readings are stable or every six weeks. Rack the wine every month until clear, then bottle.

8. Allow wine to mature for two full years from the date it was started.

Soggy Bogwater Wine

Yield 1 gallon/3.8 L

OG = 1.110 FG = 1.014 ABV = 8%

Ingredients:

- 2 lbs cranberries, fresh or frozen
- 1 lb raisins
- 3 lbs granulated sugar (about 6 ¾ cups)
- 1 campden tablet
- 1 tsp nutrients
- ¼ tsp pectic enzyme
- 1 ¼ tsp acid blend
- 1 packet wine yeast
- Water
- Standard winemaking equipment
- Nylon bag or cheesecloth
- 1-gallon carboy

Instructions:

1. Chop cranberries coarsely and place them in the cloth or bag along with the raisins. Place bag in the primary fermenter.

2. Add fruit, sugar, water, yeast nutrient, pectic enzyme, acid blend, and crushed campden tablet. Dissolve sugar by stirring well. Let sit for 24 hours.

3. Check to make sure that the SG is between 1.110 and 1.115.

4. Pitch yeast and mix in well. Stir must for five days.

5. Gently squeeze cloth to get the juice out. Rack into carboy and place airlock on the bottle.

6. For a drier tasting wine the wine should mature for at least three weeks after which the wine should be racked and allowed to mature four more weeks. The wine should be clear and the hydrometer readings stable before it is bottled.

7. For a sweeter tasting wine, mature wine for three weeks, then rack into another vessel. Dissolve ½ cup sugar in 1 cup wine and pour the sweetened wine back into the fermentation vessel. Repeat until at least two hydrometer readings are stable or every six weeks. Rack the wine every month until clear, then bottle.

8. Mature wine for a year and a half from the date it was started.

Figgy Wine

Yield 1 gallon/3.8 L

OG = 1.110 FG = 1.014 ABV = 8%

Ingredients:

- 2 lbs dried figs *
- 2 campden tablets
- 1 tsp pectic enzyme
- 2 cups honey
- 5 cups brown sugar
- 1 lemon, juice and rind
- 1 orange, juice and rind
- 1 tsp nutrients
- 1 packet wine yeast
- Water
- Standard winemaking equipment
- 1-gallon carboy
- Nylon bag or cheesecloth

Instructions:

1. In a saucepan dissolve honey in water. Bring honey water to a boil and skim off foam. Cool the honey after foam stops forming.

2. Boil a quart of water and pour it over the figs and campden tablet. Drain liquid into fermenter. Chop figs and pour another 8 cups boiling water over them with the other campden tablet. Drain liquid into fermenter. Place figs into cloth and put into fermenter. Let sit 24 hours.

3. Squeeze liquid from bag and discard. Add pectic enzyme, sugar, honey mixture, nutrients, and lemon and orange juice and rind. Pitch yeast. Make sure it makes a gallon of must by adding water.

4. In three to five days, when the active fermentation ceases, strain the wine and rack into carboy. Attach air lock.

5. For a drier tasting wine the wine should mature for at least three weeks after which the wine should be racked and allowed to mature four more weeks. The wine should be clear and the hydrometer readings stable before it is bottled.

6. For a sweeter tasting wine, mature wine for three weeks, then rack into another vessel. Dissolve ½ cup sugar in 1 cup wine and pour the sweetened wine back into the fermentation vessel. Repeat until at least two hydrometer readings are stable or every six weeks. Rack the wine every month until clear, then bottle. Bottle when the wine is ready.

7. Allow the wine to mature one year.

If you are using fresh figs, use 4 to 6 lbs.

Hot Date Wine

Yield 1 gallon/3.8 L

OG = 1.110 FG = 1.014 ABV = 8%

Ingredients:

- 4 lbs fresh dates*
- 2 campden tablets
- 5 cups white sugar or brown sugar
- 1 lemon, juice and rind
- 1 orange, juice and rind
- 1 tsp nutrients
- 1 packet wine yeast
- Water
- Standard winemaking equipment
- 1-gallon carboy
- Nylon bag or cheesecloth

Instructions:

1. Pour 8 cups boiling water over the dates. Cool. Pour liquid into fermenter. Chop dates and pour another 8 cups of hot water. Add another campden tablet. Pour liquid into fermenter.

2. Place dates in the bag/cloth. Place bag in fermenter. Let sit for 24 hours.

3. Strain the liquid from the fruit bag and discard the pulp. To the liquid add pectic enzyme, sugar, prepared honey, nutrients, and lemon and orange juice and rind and water to bring the liquid level to 1 gallon. Pitch the yeast.

4. In five days or after rapid fermentation ceases rack into carboy and attach air lock.

5. If you wish for your wine to be dry then you should allow it to mature for three weeks, rack the wine, and then allow it to mature for another four weeks. When the wine is clear and no longer needs racking, then it is ready to bottle.

6. For a sweeter tasting wine, mature wine for three weeks, then rack into another vessel. Dissolve ½ cup sugar in 1 cup wine and pour the sweetened wine back into the fermentation vessel. Repeat until at least two hydrometer readings are stable or every six weeks. Rack the wine every month until clear, then bottle. Allow wine to mature for one year after the date the batch was started.

When using dried dates only use 2 lbs of fruit.

Dinner Date Wine

Yield 1 gallon/3.8 L

OG = 1.110 FG = 1.014 ABV = 8%

Ingredients:

- 2 to 4 lbs of apples, bananas, or grapes (you may mix and match)
- 4 lbs fresh dates*
- 2 campden tablets
- 5 cups white sugar or brown sugar
- 1 lemon, juice and rind
- 1 orange, juice and rind
- 1 tsp yeast nutrient
- 1 packet yeast
- Water
- Standard winemaking equipment
- 1 gallon carboy
- Nylon bag or cheesecloth

Instructions:

1. Pour a quart of boiling water over the dates. Cool. Pour liquid into fermenter. Chop dates and pour another 8 cups of hot water. Add another campden tablet. Pour liquid into fermenter.

2. Chop other fruit and place in bag. Remove any seeds, banana peels, or stems. Crush over primary fermenter.

3. Place dates in a separate bag. Place both bags in fermenter. Let sit for 24 hours.

4. Strain the liquid from the date bag and discard the pulp. Add pectic enzyme, sugar, nutrients, and lemon and orange juice and rind. Pitch yeast and bring level to 1 gallon.

5. In five days squeeze fruit bag to get juice out. Rack into carboy and attach air lock.

6. For a drier tasting wine the wine should mature for at least three weeks after which the wine should be racked and allowed to mature four more weeks. The wine should be clear and the hydrometer readings stable before it is bottled.

7. For a sweeter tasting wine, mature wine for three weeks, then rack into another vessel. Dissolve ½ cup sugar in 1 cup wine and pour the sweetened wine back into the fermentation vessel. Repeat until at least two hydrometer readings are stable or every six weeks. Rack the wine every month until clear, then bottle.

8. Allow wine to mature for one year after the date the batch was started.

When using dried dates only use 2 lbs of fruit.

Strawberry Fields Forever Wine

Yield 1 Gallon/3.8 L

OG = 1.090 FG = 1.014 ABV = 10%

Ingredients:

- 4 to 5 pints strawberries*(fresh but not too overripe)

- 4-½ cups granulated sugar
- 1 tsp yeast nutrient
- 1 lemon, juice and rind
- 1 campden tablet
- ½-tsp pectic enzyme
- 1 packet wine yeast
- Water
- Standard winemaking equipment
- 1 gallon carboy
- Nylon bag/cheesecloth

Instructions:

1. Crush the berries in bottom of primary fermenter.

2. Add sugar, pectic enzyme, and crushed campden tablets. Stir well to dissolve sugar.

3. Create a yeast starter by adding yeast to ½ cup to 1 cup of water or orange juice, yeast nutruent and 1 tsp of sugar. Cover tightly and shake well. Allow to sit 24 hours.

4. Pitch yeast starter to berries. Stir well. Cover loosely and stir several times per day for four days. Break the hard crust that will form on top of berries daily.

5. Squeeze out as much juice as you can from the fruit and rack wine must into a carboy and attach airlock.

6. For a drier tasting wine the wine should mature for at least three weeks after which the wine should be racked and allowed to mature four more weeks. The wine should be clear and the hydrometer readings stable before it is bottled.

7. For a sweeter tasting wine, mature for three weeks, then rack into another vessel. Dissolve ½ cup sugar in 1 cup wine and pour the sweetened wine back into the fermentation vessel. Repeat every six weeks or when at least two hydrometer readings are stable. Rack the wine every month until the wine is clear, then bottle. Allow wine to mature for two full years from the date it was started.

You may use cultivated or wild strawberries or a combination of the two.

Stone Fruit Wines

These types of fruits have one large pit in them instead of many smaller seeds. These fruits also have distinct flavors and a good amount of sugar, which make them excellent candidates to be included in wine. The pits should always be removed when making a wine. These pits contain small amounts of cyanide. While a person would have to consume a great number of pits to be affected why take the chance? Often these pits can leave off flavors in wine. The easiest way to remove a pit, or stone, is to slice the fruit in half the pull the pit out.

In a couple of recipes it is recommended that the fruit is blanched. This is a quick boil that loosens the skin so that it can be removed from the pulp inside. Freezing the pulp can help you extract more juice from it.

Never use canned fruits as these contain sugar in the form of corn syrup, which does not work well in wines. They also contain preservatives that will make fermentation almost impossible.

Peachy Keen

Yield 1 Gallon/3.8 L

OG = 1.09 FG = 1.014 ABV = 10%

Ingredients:

- 2 lbs peaches
- 4 ½ cups granulated sugar
- 1 tsp yeast nutrients
- ½ tsp pectic enzyme
- ¼ tsp tannin
- 1 campden tablet
- 12 cups water, boiling
- 1 packet wine yeast
- Standard winemaking equipment
- Nylon bag/cheesecloth
- 1-gallon carboy

Instructions:

1. Removes stones and chop fruit. Place in bag/cloth. Add water, sugar, and campden tablet and bag to primary fermenter. Stir to dissolve sugar. Let sit 24 hours. Add nutrients, tannin, and pectic enzyme. Make sure the OG is between 1.090 - 1.095. Pitch yeast. Stir daily for three days.

2. Take out bag and gently squeeze out juice. Rack into carboy fermenter and attach airlock.

3. For a drier tasting wine the wine should mature for at least three weeks after which the wine should be racked and allowed to mature four more weeks. The wine should be clear and the hydrometer readings stable before it is bottled.

4. For a sweeter tasting wine, mature for three weeks, then rack into another vessel. Dissolve ½ cup sugar in 1 cup wine and pour the sweetened wine back into the fermentation vessel. Repeat every six weeks or when at least two hydrometer readings are stable. Rack the wine every month until the wine is clear, then bottle.

5. For the best results, allow the wine to mature for are least one year from the date it was started before you drink it.

Apricot Wine

Yield 1 gallon/3.8 L

OG = 1.04 FG = 1.014 ABV = 12%

Ingredients:

- 10 cups apricots, halved and pitted
- 4 ½ cups granulated sugar
- 1 tsp yeast nutrients
- 1 ½ tsp acid blend
- ½ tsp pectic enzyme
- ¼ tsp tannin
- Water
- 1 packet wine yeast
- Standard winemaking equipment
- Nylon bag/cheesecloth
- 1-gallon carboy

Instructions:

1. Place apricots in fruit bag or cheesecloth and place in primary fermenter.

2. Add hot water, sugar, nutrients, acid, pectic enzyme, tannin, and campden tablet. Make sure to stir and dissolve sugar. Let it sit 24 hours.

3. The Specific Gravity should fall between 1.090 - 1.095. Pitch the yeast. Stir daily for five to six days or until specific gravity is 1.040.

4. Gently squeeze bag. Throw away the fruit or add to your compost. Rack into carboy and add airlock.

5. If you wish to have dry wine, rack in three weeks, and again in four weeks. Continue racking every month until wine is clear. Bottle.

6. For a sweeter tasting wine, mature for three weeks, then rack into another vessel. Dissolve ½ cup sugar in 1 cup wine and pour the sweetened wine back into the fermentation vessel. Repeat every six weeks or when at least two hydrometer readings are stable. Rack the wine every month until the wine is clear, then bottle.

7. Mature the wine a year from the date you began the process.

Nectie Wine

Yield 1 Gallon/3.8 L

OG = 1.09 FG = 1.014 ABV = 10%

Ingredients:

- 2 lbs nectarines
- 4-½ cups granulated sugar
- 1 tsp yeast nutrients
- ½-tsp pectic enzyme
- ¼-tsp tannin
- 1 campden tablet
- 1 campden tablet
- 1-gallon carboy
- 1 packet wine yeast
- Cheesecloth or nylon bag
- Standard winemaking equipment

Instructions:

1. Removes stones and chop fruit. Place in bag/cloth. Add water, sugar, and campden tablet and bag to primary fermenter. Stir to dissolve sugar. Let sit 24 hours.

2. Add nutrients, tannin, and pectic enzyme. Make sure the SG is between 1.090 - 1.095. Pitch yeast. Stir daily for three days.

3. Take out bag and gently squeeze out juice. Rack into carboy fermenter and attach airlock.

4. For a drier tasting wine, the wine should mature for at least three weeks, after which the wine should be racked and allowed to mature four more weeks. The wine should be clear and the hydrometer readings stable before it is bottled.

5. For a sweeter tasting wine, mature for three weeks, then rack into another vessel. Dissolve ½ cup sugar in 1 cup wine and pour the sweetened wine back into the fermentation vessel. Repeat every six weeks or when at least two hydrometer readings are stable. Rack the wine every month until the wine is clear, then bottle.

6. Mature wine for one full year from the date it was started.

Wild Cherry Wine

Yield 1 Gallon/3.8 L

OG = 1.09 FG = 1.014 ABV = 10%

Ingredients:

- 6 lbs cherries *
- 1 lb raisins
- 5 cups granulated sugar
- 2 campden tablets
- 1 tsp nutrients
- ¾-tsp pectic enzyme
- 1 large orange (juice only)
- 1 packet wine yeast
- Nylon bag/cheesecloth
- Water
- Standard winemaking equipment
- 1-gallon carboy

Instructions:

Method 1

1. De-stem cherries and take out pits by hand. (If you have a pitter this job will be easier.)

2. Place cherries in bag/cheesecloth. Hold over fermenter and crush cherries. Place cherry bag in the primary fermenter.

3. Add enough cold water to cover fruit. Stir in pectic enzyme and campden tablets. Allow to sit for 48 hours.

4. Gently squeeze bag to get as much juice as possible. Add the rest of the ingredients except yeast. Make sure the level of liquid is 1 gallon by adding water. Make sure SG is between 1.090 and 1.110. Pitch yeast. Stir the wine must for five days or until rapid fermentation ceases.

5. Rack into carboy and attach airlock. Finish as for dry wine or sweet wine below.

Method 2

1. Remove the stems and pits from the cherries. Place fruit in a large saucepan and add enough cold water to cover. Simmer over low heat for one hour without letting it boil dry.

2. Strain the cherries out of the juice into fermentation bucket. Mix the cherry pulp with some hot water and strain the juice out of the pulp.

3. Add to primary fermenter: orange juice, sugar, campden tablets, and nutrients. Cool to mixture to about 85 degrees F/30 degrees C and add pectic enzyme. Let sit 24 hours.

4. Add water to make up to 1 gallon. Add wine yeast. Cover and stir daily for two days. Rack into carboy and attach airlock. Finish as for dry wine or sweet wine below.

Finishing

1. For a drier tasting wine the wine should mature for at least three weeks after which the wine should be racked and allowed to mature four more weeks. The wine should be clear and the hydrometer readings stable before it is bottled.

2. For a sweeter tasting wine, mature for three weeks, then rack into another vessel. Dissolve ½ cup sugar in 1 cup wine and pour the sweetened wine back into the fermentation vessel. Repeat every six weeks or when at least two hydrometer readings are stable. Rack the wine every month until the wine is clear, then bottle.

Allow wine to mature for a year and a half from the date it was started for best results.

You can use single varieties of cherries such as black cherries or bing cherries. Or you can mix different varieties for a more complex wine. You can mix sour and sweet cherries in different proportions. You can experiment with making different juices first. You can also make a sour and a sweet cherry wine and blend them after you have created them. Experiment with small quantities first.

Cherry the Wine You're With

Yield 1 Gallon/3.8 L

OG = 1.09 FG = 1.014 ABV = 10%

Ingredients:

- 8 lbs bing cherries
- 3 ½ lbs sugar
- Water

- 3 tsp pectic enzyme
- 3 campden tablets
- ½ tsp tannin
- 1 packet Premier Cuvee yeast
- Standard winemaking equipment
- Nylon bag or cheesecloth
- 1-gallon carboy

Instructions:

1. De-stem cherries and take out pits by hand. (If you have a pitter this job will be easier.) You can also stomp the cherries like grapes

2. Place cherries in bag/cheesecloth. Hold over fermenter and crush cherries. Place cherry bag in the primary fermenter.

3. Boil the remainder of the water and dissolve the sugar. Allow the water to cool and then cover the fruit with the sugar water. Stir in pectic enzyme and campden tablets. Allow to sit for 48 hours.

4. Gently squeeze bag to get as much juice as possible. Add the rest of the ingredients except yeast. Make sure that the level of liquid is 1 gallon by adding water. Make sure SG is between 1.070 and 1.110. Pitch yeast and mix in well. Stir must for five days or until rapid fermentation ceases.

5. Rack into carboy and attach airlock.

6. For a drier tasting wine the wine should mature for at least three weeks after which the wine should be racked and allowed to mature four more weeks. The wine should be clear and the hydrometer readings stable before it is bottled.

7. For a sweeter tasting wine, mature for three weeks, then rack into

another vessel. Dissolve ½ cup sugar in 1 cup wine and pour the sweetened wine back into the fermentation vessel. Repeat every six weeks or when at least two hydrometer readings are stable. Rack the wine every month until the wine is clear, then bottle.

8. Mature the wine for a year and a half from the date it was started.

Do not throw the fruit in the cheesecloth away. This is referred to as pomace and can be used to make cherry mead in Chapter 8.

Chokecherries are a small type of cherry and are not usually available in supermarkets. They should not be mistaken for chokeberries. You can find this type of bird cherry in North America. They are not found in the southern-most and northern-most states. They grow on a small bush or tree about five meters tall. The flowers grow in late spring. The mature ones are bright red, about 1 centimeter in diameter. They have an astringent, sour taste.

Chokecherry Wine

Yield 1 Gallon/3.8 L

OG = 1.100 FG = 1.014 ABV = 12%

Ingredients:

- 2 lbs choke cherries
- 1 lb raisins
- 5 cups granulated sugar
- 1 campden tablets
- 1 tsp nutrients
- ½ tsp pectic enzyme
- 1 large lemon (juice only)
- 1 packet wine yeast
- Water
- Standard wine equipment
- 1-gallon carboy
- Nylon bag/cheesecloth

Instructions:

1. Wash cherries and place them in the bag. Crush over the primary fermenter. Break the skin of every fruit but be careful so you do not break any of the pits. Place fruit bag in the primary fermenter. Add water to cover the bag. Stir in campden tablet and pectic enzyme. Allow mixture to sit for 24 hours.

2. Place the rest of the ingredients in the fermenter with the exception the yeast. Once the SG is between 1.100 and 1.110 pitch the yeast and mix in well. Cover primary fermenter. Stir daily for five to six days, until rapid fermentation ceases.

3. Remove the bag and gently squeeze out the juice. Rack into carboy.

4. For a drier tasting wine the wine should mature for at least three weeks after which the wine should be racked and allowed to mature four more weeks. The wine should be clear and the hydrometer readings stable before it is bottled.

5. For a sweeter tasting wine, mature for three weeks, then rack into another vessel. Dissolve ½ cup sugar in 1 cup wine and pour the sweetened wine back into the fermentation vessel. Repeat every six weeks or when at least two hydrometer readings are stable. Rack the wine every month until the wine is clear, then bottle.

6. Mature the wine for a year and a half from the date it was started.

This recipe won first prize for a fruit wine in the North Carolina State Fair 2002 wine competition. I had bought a number of juicy plums for the grocery store. I took them home, cut and removed the stones, and then I squeezed each plum by hand. I sent two bottles to Raleigh for the state fair wine competition. I was not able to attend, but to my surprise, I received a letter and a check in the mail. I had won first place in the non-grape wine competition. I was so excited, and it only added to my obsession to create more wine at home.

I have recreated this wine many years since, but none of them quite had the sweet taste of victory like the wine I made that first year.

Plum Winner

Yield 1 Gallon/3.8 L

OG = 1.100 FG = 1.014 ABV = 12%

Ingredients

- 5 lbs fully ripened plums
- Water
- 2 ½ lbs of sugar or honey
- 1 ½ tsp of acid blend
- ⅛ tsp of tannin
- 1 tsp yeast nutrient
- Pectic enzyme
- 1 packet of yeast (champagne or Montracet is recommended. You may use sweet mead yeast especially if you are using honey.)

- 1 campden tablet, crushed and dissolved
- Fining agent per manufacturer's instructions
- Standard wine equipment
- 1-gallon carboy
- Nylon bag/cheesecloth

Instructions

1. Cut plums in half and remove the pits. Leave the skins. Crush the fruits by hand. Some plums can be hard so you can put them in a fruit grinder if you have one. Squeeze the juice out of the plums, and place the plums in the bag or cheesecloth. Place bag in the fermenter. Boil a half-gallon of water and dissolve the sugar in it by stirring. If you are using honey then skim any foam that forms on the top. Add a half-gallon of water and sugar water to the

fermentation bucket. Allow the liquid to cool to room temperature and then add tannin, yeast nutrient, and campden tablet.

2. Your total acid test should read about 0.65 to 0.75. If it is already at this level you will not need to add any additional acid blend. If it is lower than you should add the acid blend. If the TA is too high you can add some water and sugar to adjust the acidity. Try to avoid dilution if possible. Allow the fermenter to sit for 12 hours. Add pectic enzyme according to manufacturer's instructions. Allow must to sit another 24 hours.

3. Take a sanitized smasher and crush the fruit. I have found that a potato masher is great to use. Pitch the yeast.

4. Stir daily until the SG reaches 1.040 or the active fermentation has ceased. Remove the bag and gently squeeze out the juice. Discard the remaining fruit pulp.

5. Allow the wine settle in another week. Rack to secondary fermenter. You may wish to add a campden tablet.

6. After two weeks rack again. Add water to raise the level back to a gallon. You may add a campden tablet.

7. Allow to sit for another two to six months. You may want to rack the wine monthly.

8. Once the wine has begun to clear and the SG levels are stabilized you may add a stabilizer and clarifier.

9. I have found that plum wine is best a little sweetened. You may add about 2 to 6 ounces of sugar in a little water to taste.

10. When you are sure the wine has stabilized, you may bottle it. Allow wine to mature from six to 12 months. This wine improves greatly with age.

Seeded Fruits

There is no technical group of fruits called seeded fruits, but I organized them according to fruits that have a lot of seeds in them. Some of these come from trees and others from vines. Most of these require you remove the seeds before they are used in a wine. Many times this is done by hand. If the seeds are small and intact they may be used in a wine and then discarded when the wine is racked. The important thing is that the seeds not be broken, so that off flavors to not leech into the wine.

Kiwi Bird Wine

Yield 1 Gallon/3.8 L

OG = 1.100 FG = 1.014 ABV = 12%

Ingredients:

- 6 cups chopped kiwi
- 1 ½ cups light raisins
- 4 ½ cups granulated sugar
- 2 oranges, juice only
- 1 campden tablet
- 1 tsp pectic enzyme
- ½ tsp nutrients
- ½ tsp energizer
- Water
- 1 packet wine yeast
- Standard winemaking equipment
- 1-gallon carboy

Instructions:

1. Put all of the ingredients in the primary fermenter except the yeast. Make sure the liquid reaches 1 gallon by adding cold water. Let sit

24 hours.

2. Pitch yeast. Leave for five days, stirring daily until rapid fermentation ceases.

3. Rack into carboy. Top off with water. Attach airlock.

4. Rack after three weeks. Return wine to carboy.

5. For a drier tasting wine the wine should mature for at least three weeks after which the wine should be racked and allowed to mature four more weeks. The wine should be clear and the hydrometer readings stable before it is bottled.

6. For a sweeter tasting wine, mature for three weeks, then rack into another vessel. Dissolve ½-cup sugar in 1 cup wine and pour the sweetened wine back into the fermentation vessel. Repeat every six weeks or when at least two hydrometer readings are stable. Rack the wine every month until the wine is clear, then bottle.

7. Allow the wine to mature a year for the best results.

Walter Melon Wine

Yield 1 Gallon/3.8 L

OG = 1.100 FG = 1.014 ABV = 12%

Ingredients:

- 8 cups watermelon juice (seedless varieties work better)
- ⅛ tsp tannin
- 3-½ cups granulated sugar
- 2 campden tablets
- 1 tsp nutrients
- 2 ½ tsps acid blend
- 1 packet wine yeast
- 8 cups water

- Standard winemaking equipment

Instructions:

1. Remove rind and cube the watermelon flesh. Blend the cubes in a food processor or blender. Pour into the primary fermenter. Add all other ingredients except the yeast. Stir well to dissolve sugar. Let sit for 24 hours.

2. Make sure the SG is between 1.090 and 1.100. Add yeast and mix in well. Cover primary fermenter. Stir mixture for five days.

3. Rack into carboy and attach airlock.

4. If you wish for your wine to be dry then you should allow it to mature for three weeks, rack the wine, and then allow it to mature for another four weeks. When the wine is clear and no longer needs racking, then it is ready to bottle.

5. For a sweeter tasting wine, mature for three weeks and then rack into another vessel. Dissolve ½-cup sugar in 1 cup of wine and pour the sweetened wine back into the fermentation vessel. Repeat this process until at least two hydrometer readings are stable, or every six weeks. Rack the wine every month until the wine is clear, then bottle.

6. Allow wine to mature for a year and a half from the date it was started.

You may want to try a seedless watermelon. The seeds could impart a slight bitter flavor depending on the watermelon and how ripe it is.

Sunny Melon Wine

Yield 1 Gallon/3.8 L

OG = 1.100 FG = 1.014 ABV = 10%

Ingredients:

- 4 lbs melon (honeydew, muskmelon, cantaloupe, or whatever melons you like. You can mix and match if you like.)
- 6 ½ cups sugar
- 2 lemons
- 2 oranges
- 1 tsp pectic enzyme
- 1 tsp nutrients
- 3 campden tablets
- 1 packet wine yeast
- Water
- Nylon bag or cheesecloth
- 1-gallon carboy
- Standard winemaking equipment

Instructions:

1. Cut and scoop out the flesh of the melon. Add the seeds and flesh of melon and sliced lemons and oranges (with seeds removed) to the bag/cloth. Add crushed campden tablets, sugar, nutrients, and bag to fermenter. Pour a quart of boiling water over the fruit. Stir to dissolve, cover, and let sit 24 hours.

2. Make sure the SG is about 1.100. Add pectic enzyme and pitch the yeast. Stir daily for five days.

3. Remove bag and strain and rack liquid to put liquid into carboy. Add water to make up to 1 gallon. Attach an airlock.

4. For a drier tasting wine the wine, mature for at least three weeks, then rack and allow to mature four more weeks. The wine should be clear and the hydrometer readings stable before it is bottled.

5. For a sweeter tasting wine, mature for three weeks and then rack into another vessel. Dissolve ½ cup sugar in 1 cup of wine and pour the sweetened wine back into the fermentation vessel. Repeat this process until at least two hydrometer readings are stable, or every six weeks. Rack the wine every month until the wine is clear, then bottle.

6. Mature wine for a year and a half from the date it was started.

Underworld Wine

Yield 1 Gallon/3.8 L

OG = 1.090 FG = 1.014 ABV = 10%

Ingredients:

- 6 pomegranates (ripe and juicy)*
- 1 lb raisins
- 4 cups granulated sugar
- 2 tsp acid blend
- 1 tsp pectic enzyme
- 1 tsp yeast nutrient
- 1 campden tablet
- 1 packet wine yeast
- Water
- Standard winemaking equipment
- 1-gallon carboy
- Nylon bag/cheesecloth

Instructions:

1. Cut open pomegranates. Put seeds in bag/cloth. Do not get any pith or skin. Be careful as the fruit is around the outside seeds, so it is a good idea to do this over the fermenter so you will not lose

any juice. Crush the fruit and place bag in fermenter. Add a quart of water and all other ingredients except the yeast. Stir the sugar vigorously in order to dissolve. Let sit 24 hours.

2. Make sure the SG is between 1.090 and 1.095. Pitch the yeast and stir. Stir for six days or until specific gravity is 1.050.

3. Gently squeeze bag. Be careful not to allow too much tannin to escape from the seeds. Rack into carboy and attach airlock.

4. For a drier tasting wine, mature for at least three weeks, then rack and allow to mature four more weeks. The wine should be clear and the hydrometer readings stable before it is bottled.

5. For a sweeter tasting wine, mature for three weeks and then rack into another vessel. Dissolve ½ cup sugar in 1 cup of wine and pour the sweetened wine back into the fermentation vessel. Repeat this process until at least two hydrometer readings are stable, or every six weeks. Rack the wine every month until the wine is clear, then bottle.

6. For the best results allow the wine to age for at least a year before drinking.

Pomegranates can be found in different sizes. Be aware that by using six large fruits you will have a fuller-bodied wine, but using smaller fruit will not take as long to age. Make sure the fruit is not dry. Use the juiciest fruit you can find.

A Wine Pearing

Yield 1 Gallon/3.8 L

OG = 1.100 FG = 1.014 ABV = 12%

Ingredients:

- 12 cups pears, chopped
- 1 lb raisins
- 6 cups granulated sugar*
- 1 ½ tsp acid blend
- 1 campden tablet
- ½ tsp pectic enzyme
- 1 tsp nutrients
- Water
- 1 packet wine yeast
- Standard winemaking equipment
- Nylon Bag/cheesecloth
- 1-gallon carboy

Instructions:

1. Cube pears and remove the core. Add sugar, pectic enzyme, and crushed campden tablets. Stir well to dissolve sugar.

2. Create a yeast starter by adding yeast to ½ cup to 1 cup of water or orange juice, yeast nutrient and 1 tsp of sugar. Cover tightly and shake well. Allow to sit 24 hours.

3. Pitch yeast starter to berries. Stir well. Cover loosely and stir several times per day for four days. Break the hard crust that will form on top of fruit daily.

4. Squeeze out as much juice as you can from the fruit and rack wine must into a carboy and attach airlock.

5. For a drier tasting wine, mature for at least three weeks, then rack and allow to mature four more weeks. The wine should be clear and the hydrometer readings stable before it is bottled.

6. For a sweeter tasting wine, mature for three weeks and then rack into another vessel. Dissolve ½ cup sugar in 1 cup of wine and pour the sweetened wine back into the fermentation vessel. Repeat this process until at least two hydrometer readings are stable, or every six weeks. Rack the wine every month until it is clear, then bottle.

7. Allow wine to mature for two full years from the date it was started.

*You can replace sugar with 7 cups brown sugar or 6 cups honey.

A Second Pair of Pears

Yield 5 gallons/19 L

OG = 1.100 FG = 1.014 ABV = 12%

Ingredients:

- 20 lbs pears
- 10 lbs granulated sugar
- ½ tsp pectic enzyme
- Water
- Packet of EC-1118 yeast
- Cheesecloth or nylon bag
- Carboy
- 1 tbsp yeast energizer
- ½ tsp wine tannin
- 3 tbsp of acid blend
- Standard winemaking equipment

Instructions:

1. Cube pears. Add sugar, pectic enzyme, and crushed campden tablets. Stir well to dissolve sugar.

2. Create a yeast starter by adding yeast ½ cup to 1 cup of water or orange juice, yeast nutrient and 1 tsp of sugar. Add water to 5-gallon level, cover tightly and shake well. Allow to sit 24 hours.

3. Pitch yeast starter to fruit. Stir well. Cover loosely and stir several times per day for four days. Break the hard crust that will form on

top of berries daily.

4. Squeeze out as much juice as you can from the fruit and rack wine must into a carboy and attach airlock.

5. For a drier tasting wine, mature for at least three weeks, then rack and allow to mature four more weeks. The wine should be clear and the hydrometer readings stable before it is bottled.

6. For a sweeter tasting wine, mature for three weeks and then rack into another vessel. Dissolve ½-cup sugar in 1 cup of wine and pour the sweetened wine back into the fermentation vessel. Repeat this process until at least two hydrometer readings are stable, or every six weeks. Rack the wine every month until it is clear, then bottle.

7. Allow wine to mature for two full years from the date it was started.

Citrus Fruits

I grew up in Florida with orange, grapefruit, and tangerine trees in my backyard. I loved picking the fruit straight from the tree. There was nothing to compare to fresh fruit juice directly from the source.

I visited Florida a number of years ago and came across a winery, Florida Orange Groves Inc & Winery. This was my first experience tasting citrus wines. It was amazing to taste the flavors of orange and grapefruit that came through. I was so excited, I wrote an article about citrus wines for *WineMaker* magazine, but the owner would not reveal his secret process of creating wine that tastes just like you picked an orange off the tree. Through experimentation I was able to come up with recipes that work well and brought back the images of sandy beaches and orange groves from my youth.

> Making grapefruit wine is all about getting the acid down and the sugar up while extracting enough color and flavor to have a drinkable wine, but without getting too much bitterness. The end result is tasty on its own, but is also very good as a mixer with other alcohols such as vodka, or with tonic water.
> *Chris Minnick, Bad Astronauts Winery of Sacramento*

2008 Galactic Grapefruit

Yield 1 Gallon/3.8L

OG = 1.010 FG = 1.001 ABV = 10%

Ingredients:

- 5 grapefruit
- Water
- 2 ¼ lbs sugar
- 1 campden tablet
- ¼ tsp grape tannin
- Standard winemaking equipment
- Nylon bag/cheesecloth

Instructions:

1. Peel and segment the grapefruit. Put the segments into a nylon bag/cheesecloth. Be careful to get as little of the white part of the peel in the bag as possible. Put the zest of one grapefruit into the bag too. Put the nylon bag into a fermenter. Add the water, sugar, crushed Camden tablet, and tannin. Stir until everything is well mixed. Let it sit for 24 hours.

2. Grapefruit must does not start fermenting easily. Get the strongest yeast you can (I use Lalvin EC-1118 Champagne yeast), follow the

manufacturer's instructions, and pitch after 24 hours with 5 grams for up to 5 gallons, and 1 gram per gallon thereafter.

3. Ferment the wine to dry, stirring and squeezing the bag of grapefruit once per day. When the wine is dry, or nearly dry, remove the bags of grapefruit and rack the wine into glass carboy. Let it finish fermenting for three to four months. Rack again, and then let it sit for another three months.

4. Filter using the following sequence of filters: course, polish, then sterile. The course filtration will not be easy and you will likely go through several sets of filter pads.

5. To make grapefruit wine drinkable, you need to add sugar before bottling. If you want to take a risk that your filtration actually was sterile, just do bench trials to determine how much sugar is correct (I use about ¼ lb per gallon). If you want to play it safe and make sure your wine is not going to start fermenting in the bottle (I do), add ½ tsp potassium sorbate dissolved in a small amount of water at least ½ hour prior to adding the sugar.

6. After adding the sugar, bottle the wine and let it sit for several months before enjoying!

Florida Grapefruit Wine

Yield 1 Gallon/3.8 L

OG = 1.010 FG = 1.001 ABV = 10%

Ingredients:

- 6 large grapefruit
- 3 lbs cane sugar
- Water
- ½ tsp. pectic enzyme
- ⅛ tsp tannin

- 1 crushed campden tablet
- Fining agent
- Wine yeast
- ½ tsp potassium sorbate
- Standard winemaking equipment

Instructions:

1. Squeeze all the juice from the grapefruits using a reamer, and remove any peel or seeds. Set aside the peel and juiced pulp from one of the grapefruits. Remove the pith from the inside of the peel; add the peel to the juice along with 1 ½ lbs sugar, the campden tablet, tannin, and yeast nutrient. Add enough water to top off the mixture at the 1-gallon mark.

2. Make sure the sugar is dissolved in the mixture by stirring vigorously. Add the pulp that was set aside. Allow the mixture to sit 12 to 18 hours covered.

3. Add the pectic enzyme and allow the juice to sit for another 12 hours.

4. Pitch the yeast. Allow the must to ferment for two days and then add sugar. Make sure it is stirred well to dissolve the sugar. Allow the must to ferment for another four to five days.

5. Strain out the peel and pulp and then rack the must into a carboy. Add fining agents to clarify wine.

6. For a drier tasting wine, mature for at least three weeks, then rack and allow maturing four more weeks. The wine should be clear and the hydrometer readings stable before it is bottled.

7. For a sweeter tasting wine, mature for three weeks and then rack into another vessel. Dissolve ½ cup sugar in 1 cup of wine and pour the sweetened wine back into the fermentation vessel. Repeat this process until at least two hydrometer readings are stable, or every six weeks. Rack the wine every month until it is clear, then bottle.

8. Allow wine to mature for at least six months.

Tropical Fruits

Think of the islands and Tiki bars. These wines are full of sunshine, days lounging by the pool, and sipping Pina Coladas. These wines are best sweet and served during an outdoor barbecue. These flavors also remind me of Florida. I can remember going out into the Gulf with friends at sunset and watching the sun melt into the ocean while drinking a Bahama Mama or a Tequila Sunrise.

Pineapple Wine

Yield 1 Gallon/3.8 L

OG = 1.090 FG = 1.001 ABV = 10%

Ingredients:

- 3 lbs fresh pineapple *
- 1 campden tablet
- 4 cups white sugar
- 1 tsp nutrients
- ¼ tsp tannin
- 1 packet wine yeast
- Water
- Standard winemaking equipment
- 1-gallon carboy
- Nylon bag/cheesecloth

Instructions:

1. Cut the top from pineapple and peel it. Cut the pineapple into quarters lengthwise and remove the core. Chop into small pieces and place in bag/cloth. Place bag into fermentation bucket. Add quart of water and all other ingredients except the yeast. Let sit 24 hours.

2. Be sure the SG is between 1.090 and 1.095. Pitch yeast. Stir daily until rapid fermentation ceases.

3. Remove the bag and gently squeeze juice out. Rack into carboy.

Attach air lock.

4. For a drier wine, allow it to mature for three weeks, rack the wine, and then allow it to mature for another four weeks. When the wine is clear and no longer needs racking, it is ready to bottle.

5. For a sweeter tasting wine, mature for three weeks and then rack into another vessel. Dissolve ½ cup sugar in 1 cup of wine and pour the sweetened wine back into the fermentation vessel. Repeat this process until at least two hydrometer readings are stable, or every six weeks. Rack the wine every month until it is clear, then bottle.

6. Mature the wine one year after the date the batch was started.

When weighing your pineapples at the store account for about ½ lb of waste per pineapple. Do not use canned pineapple due to added sugar and preservatives.

Golden Sunshine

Yield 5 gallons/19 L

OG = 1.090 FG = 1.001 ABV = 10%

Ingredients:

- 15 lbs pineapple
- 9 lbs granulated sugar
- ½ tsp pectic enzyme
- Water
- Packet of Montrachet yeast
- Standard winemaking equipment
- Cheesecloth or nylon bag
- Carboy
- 1 tbsp yeast energizer
- 1 tsp wine tannin
- 2 tsp of acid blend

Instructions:

1. Cut the top from pineapple and peel it. Cut the pineapple into quarters lengthwise and remove the core. Chop into small pieces and

place in bag/cloth. Place bag into fermentation bucket. Add quart of water and all other ingredients except the yeast. Let sit 24 hours.

2. Be sure the SG is between 1.090 and 1.095. Raise level of water to 5 gallons and pitch yeast. Stir daily until rapid fermentation ceases.

3. Remove the bag and gently squeeze juice out. Rack into carboy. Attach air lock.

4. For a drier tasting wine the wine should mature for at least three weeks after which the wine should be racked and allowed to mature four more weeks. The wine should be clear and the hydrometer readings stable before it is bottled.

5. For a sweeter tasting wine, mature for three weeks and then rack into another vessel. Dissolve ½ cup sugar in 1 cup of wine and pour the sweetened wine back into the fermentation vessel. Repeat this process until at least two hydrometer readings are stable, or every six weeks. Rack the wine every month until it is clear, then bottle.

6. Mature the wine one year after the date the batch was started.

Monkey Wine

Yield 1 Gallon/3.8 L
OG = 1.04 FG = 1.014 ABV = 10%

Ingredients:

- 3 lbs ripe bananas
  (do not use green bananas)
- 1 ½ cups light raisins
- 5 cups granulated sugar
- 2 juiced lemons
- 1 tsp nutrients
- Water
- 1 packet wine yeast

- 2 campden tablets
- 1-gallon carboy
- Standard winemaking equipment

Instructions:

1. Peel and cut bananas into slices. Reserve and cube half of the banana peels. Place both in a large saucepan with 6 cups water. Bring bananas and peels to a boil. Simmer the mixture for 30 minutes. Strain out fruit and peel.

2. Mix raisins, sugar, campden tablets, and the lemon juice in the primary fermenter. Pour hot banana liquid over sugar mixture. Stir the mixture to dissolve the sugar. Fill the fermenter to the 1-gallon mark with cold water. Let it sit for 24 hours.

3. Add nutrients and pitch the yeast. Stir must for five days.

4. Siphon into carboy and attach airlock.

5. For a drier tasting wine, mature for at least three weeks, then rack and allow to mature four more weeks. The wine should be clear and the hydrometer readings stable before it is bottled.

6. For a sweeter tasting wine, mature for three weeks and then rack into another vessel. Dissolve ½ cup sugar in 1 cup of wine and pour the sweetened wine back into the fermentation vessel. Repeat this process until at least two hydrometer readings are stable, or every six weeks. Rack the wine every month until it is clear, then bottle.

Crazy Monkey Wine

Yield 1 Gallon/3.8 L

OG = 1.04 FG = 1.014 ABV = 10%

Ingredients:

- 3 lbs ripe bananas (do not use green bananas)
- 1 ½ cups light raisins
- 5 cups brown sugar
- 2 lemons juiced
- 1 oz bruised ginger root
- 1 oz whole cloves
- 1- to 4-inch cinnamon stick
- 2 campden tablets
- 1 tsp nutrients
- Water
- 1 packet wine yeast
- 1-gallon carboy
- Standard winemaking equipment

Instructions:

1. Peel and cut bananas into slices. Reserve and cube half of the banana peels. Place both in a large saucepan with 6 cups water. Bring bananas and peels to a boil. Simmer the mixture for 30 minutes. Strain out fruit and peel.

2. Mix sugar, raisins, cinnamon, ginger root, clove, campden tablets, and the lemon juice in the primary fermenter. Pour hot banana liquid over sugar mixture. Stir the mixture to dissolve the sugar. Fill the fermenter to the 1-gallon mark with cold water. Let it sit for 24 hours.

3. Add nutrients and pitch the yeast. Stir must for five days.

4. Siphon into carboy and attach airlock.

5. For a drier tasting wine, mature for at least three weeks, then rack and allow to mature four more weeks. The wine should be clear and the hydrometer readings stable before it is bottled.

6. For sweet wine, rack at three weeks. Add ½ cup sugar dissolved in 1 cup of wine. Stir gently, and place back into carboy. Repeat process every six weeks until specific gravity is stable. Rack every month until wine is clear. Bottle when wine is ready.

CASE STUDY: DAVE SCHIEDERMAYER

schieds@att.net
Home winemaker

I have made wine, cider, and beer for several years as a hobby. I enjoy winemaking because it allows me to use biology and chemistry in order to create fine drink. My friend John La Puma, who is an excellent chef and winemaker, got me interested in making cider from all the apples my dad and mom had on their land.

My favorite wine that I have created is called Morgan Arnold, which is in honor my father in law. It is made with good old-fashioned Concord grape juice. My favorite wild wine is Mabe's tomato citrus wine, made from my mother-in-law's homegrown tomatoes. I won a blue ribbon at the Wisconsin stage fair for my cider.

To me, a basic wine kit should include siphon hoses, a magic siphon or two, a wine thief or two, long plastic spoons, a pH meter and an osmometer, acid blend, tannin, sulfite tablets, lots of juices and sugars as needed, and glass carboys, I prefer 5 gallons since they are lighter, as well as some plastic fermentation jugs. Old liquid malt containers are 15 gallons and are cheap and food grade quality so they can be used for primary fermenters.

One tip I would give to new winemakers is to ferment wine in the cool downstairs far away from the furnace in the still dark cavern like part of the basement. For those looking for the right food to go with their wild wine I would suggest pizza.

Apple Cider

There is a rich history of making apple wine or cider in the United States and Britain. In England during the medieval times, cider was used to pay workers at the monasteries. This practice continued until recently. Before settling America, cider making began to decline in England and throughout Europe. This was due to poor crops and other agricultural issues.

The United States was a totally different issue. Apple seeds were brought to the New World in order to grow orchards. Cider became the most popular drink in the colonies. Consumption of cider increased until the prohibition in 1919. More recently, cider has made resurgence in both England and America.

Cider is different than apple juice, which is filtered and usually pasteurized. All the life is removed from apple juice, so it is not recommended that you use it. It may also contain high amounts of sulfites that could make fermentation close to impossible.

The best places to get good cider are at roadside stands near orchards. You need to check if the cider has been pasteurized. It is better if it is not, but you can still use it. The best way to make cider is to press the apples yourself. First they must be macerated and then they can be pressed.

I have gone through the process a few times. It is totally worth the mess and the bees to make your own cider. It turns a brown color because of oxidation, but this is totally normal. The finished product will be a pale golden color.

Cider can be dry, sweet, or sparkling. If you are really adventurous, you can try your hand at creating applejack, which is essentially apple whiskey. It does take distilling, which is not legal without a permit. There is another way to make applejack using a freezing technique. In fact, applejack was made in colonial times by "jacking" or freezing hard cider. Hard cider is another name for apple wine. I only present the method here for consideration. I am in no way advocating freeze distillation if it is illegal where you live. You will need to check with you local laws considering it. Check online under your local ATF (Alcohol, Tobacco, and Firearms) or ALE (Alcohol Law Enforcement) divisions.

The process is simple. Alcohol does not freeze at the same temperature that water does. If you place vodka in your freezer it will not freeze. However, beer, which has high water content, will freeze. When cider is frozen, it is the water that freezes. Inside this casing of water is alcohol. Place a bucket in your freezer and allow it to sit there for a week, so that it will freeze solid. Take a sterilized ice pick or similar device and make a hole in the ice that forms. Then pour the liquid out of the ice block into a bottle. You may want to use a funnel for this. You can then throw out the remaining ice. The liquid inside will be concentrated apple liquor.

If the temperature is freezing outside, run water through the pipes so they do not burst. Water does a funny thing that other liquids do not — it expands. Most other liquids near the freezing point contract or become more compact. If you do not use a vessel that is large enough to allow the water in the cider to expand, it will crack and burst.

If you are not sure that your applejack is condensed enough the first time, you can pour the liquid from within the ice into another container. Allow this liquid to freeze and repeat the process. I will again stress this process may not be legal where you are located, as it is a form of distillation. In the wine drinks section I have given you a recipe to create your own form of applejack without the necessity of home distillation.

Hard Cider Rules

Yield 5 gallons/19 L

OG = 1.040 FG = 1.001 ABV = 10%

Ingredients:

- 5 gallons of cider
- 5 lbs of cane sugar
- 2 tbsp of yeast nutrient
- ½ tsp of pectic enzyme
- 2 ½ tsp of acid blend
- 1 tsp of wine tannin
- 1 tsp of ascorbic acid
- 1 campden tablet
- 1 Packet Lalvin EC-1118 yeast
- Standard winemaking equipment
- Fruit crusher
- Fruit press
- Cheesecloth for the press

Instructions:

1. It takes about 14 to 16 lbs of apples, or 36 apples, to make a gallon of cider. You will need about a bushel and a half of apples to make 5 gallons of cider. Make sure you inspect the apples and cut off bad spots or discard bad apples. Wash and gently scrub the apples. You will then next to macerate, or break down the whole apple, core and all into a mush. You can do this with a fruit crusher or in a pinch you can use a food processer. You will need a press to extract the juice from the pulp.

2. Mix all of ingredients in the primary fermenter except the yeast. Place a towel over the top of the fermenter and allow sit for 24 hours.

3. Pitch yeast. Seal and attach air lock.

4. Allow rapid fermentation to continue for about a week. When it slows down and the SG reading is about 1.030, rack into secondary fermenter. Attach air lock.

5. Continue to fermenter for a month. When the SG reads 0.998 or less rack into another vessel. Add a campden tablet.

6. Allow cider to continue to settle and clear for another three weeks. When the cider is clear and the hydrometer readings are stable, rack to bottling bucket and add another campden tablet.

7. If you wish to create a sweeter cider, then you will allow the cider to mature three weeks and then rack it into another carboy. Dissolve ½ cup sugar in 1 cup of cider. Add this sweetened cup of wine to the carboy. You will need to repeat this process until wine is clear. Bottle when the wine is ready.

8. Allow the cider to mature for about three months or longer for the best taste.

The second president of the United States, John Adams, drank a tankard of cider every morning with breakfast. It must have given him long life, because he lived to age 91.

CHAPTER 4

Vegetable Wines

As we move away from fruits to vegetables, you may be skeptical whether these types of wines taste good. Vegetables come from plants just like fruits, and they contain natural sugars, just like fruits. They do not contain as much sugar as an apple or banana, so you will add more sugar. This is not only to balance the taste but also to bring up the potential alcohol content of your wine. There are liquors made from corn and potatoes and neither vodka nor corn whiskey taste like buttered corn or a baked potato. Give these wild wines a chance. Their flavors can be subtle but delicious.

> Prickly pear cactus actually has two edible parts: the cactus pads and the nopales, or prickly pear fruit. The pads are similar to okra as they become a little sticky when cooked. The pads taste like green bean, asparagus, or green pepper.

The nopales are 2 to 4 inches long and look a little like an avocado. The color of a ripe prickly pear can be anything from yellow or orange to magenta or red. You have to be careful of the small prickly spines in the prickly pear's skin as these can be irritating to skin and cause digestive upset if ingested. The fruit on the inside can range in color from yellow to dark red. It is sweet and juicy and crunchy seeds can be found throughout it.

Prickly Wine

Yield 1 Gallon/3.8 L

OG = 1.100 FG = 1.014 ABV = 12%

Ingredients:

- 12 cups prepared prickly pears (ripe fruit)
- 1 ¼ cups raisins
- 4 ½ cups granulated sugar
- 1 campden tablets
- ¾ tsp yeast energizer
- 1 tsp pectic enzyme
- 2 lemons (juice only)
- 1 packet wine yeast
- 4 cups water
- Standard winemaking equipment
- 1-gallon carboy

Instructions:

1. Be very careful and remove spines from fruit. I suggest using gloves. Chop, crush, and place them in the primary fermenter. Add the rest of the ingredients except the yeast. Make sure the SG is between 1.100 and 1.110. Pitch yeast and mix in well. Stir daily for five to six days, until rapid fermentation ceases.

2. Pull out bag and gently squeeze out the juice. Rack into carboy.

3. For a drier tasting wine, mature for at least three weeks, then rack and allow to mature four more weeks. The wine should be clear and the hydrometer readings stable before it is bottled.

4. For a sweeter tasting wine, mature for three weeks and then rack into another vessel. Dissolve ½ cup sugar in 1 cup of wine and pour the sweetened wine back into the fermentation vessel. Repeat this process until at least two hydrometer readings are stable, or every six weeks. Rack the wine every month until it is clear, then bottle.

5. Mature the wine for a year and a half from the date it was started.

> When choosing rhubarb, choose the reddest stalks possible. This gives the wine a nice pale red color. Be careful and do not use any of the rhubarb leaves, as they are poisonous.

BackRhub Wine

Yield 1 Gallon/ 3.8 L

OG = 1.100 FG = 1.014 ABV = 12%

Ingredients:

- 10 to 12 cups rhubarb, sliced thinly
- 1- to 4-inch cinnamon stick
- 7 cups granulated sugar*
- 2 campden tablets
- 1 tsp nutrients
- ½ tsp pectic enzyme
- 1 packet wine yeast
- Water
- Standard winemaking equipment
- 1-gallon carboy
- Nylon bag/cheesecloth

Instructions:

1. Pour water into primary fermenter. Add campden tablet and pectic enzyme. Stir well. Place the rhubarb in the bag/cloth and put in fermenter. Let sit for 48 hours. Stir daily.

2. Remove bag but do not squeeze. Stir while dissolving sugar and nutrients in the liquid. Make sure the SG is between 1.100 and 1.110. Pitch yeast and stir into must. Let sit 24 hours overnight.

3. Rack into carboy, add cinnamon stick, and attach airlock.

4. For a drier tasting wine, mature for at least three weeks, then rack and allow to mature four more weeks. The wine should be clear and the hydrometer readings stable before it is bottled.

5. For a sweeter tasting wine, mature for three weeks and then rack into another vessel. Dissolve ½ cup sugar in 1 cup of wine and pour the sweetened wine back into the fermentation vessel. Repeat this process until at least two hydrometer readings are stable, or every six weeks. Rack the wine every month until it is clear, then bottle.

6. Allow wine to mature for a year and a half from the date it was started.

You may substitute brown sugar in place of the white sugar.

Denmark Wine

Yield 1 Gallon/3.8 L

OG = 1.100 FG = 1.014 ABV = 12%

Ingredients:

- 5 cups Brussels sprouts
- 1 cup raisins
- 6 ½ cups granulated sugar
- 1 tsp yeast nutrients
- 2 lemons
- 1 campden tablet
- Water
- 1 packet wine yeast
- Standard winemaking equipment
- 1 gallon carboy
- Nylon bag/cheesecloth

Instructions:

1. Bring water to a boil. Shred Brussels sprouts and place in bag/cloth along with raisins. Place bag in primary fermenter. Pour boiling water into fermenter. Add sugar, stirring to dissolve. Let sit 24 hours.

2. Be sure that the SG is between 1.090 and 1.100. Slice the whole lemon, rind and all and add to primary. Add the remaining ingredients, including the yeast. Stir daily for five days as fermentation begins.

3. Remove bag and gently squeeze. Rack into secondary fermenter and attach airlock.

4. For a drier tasting wine, the wine should mature for at least three weeks after which the wine should be racked and allowed to mature four more weeks. The wine should be clear and the hydrometer readings stable before it is bottled.

5. For a sweet wine, rack at three weeks. Add ½ cup sugar dissolved in 1 cup wine. Stir gently, and place back into carboy. Repeat process every six weeks until specific gravity is stable. Rack every month until wine is clear. Bottle when the wine is ready.

6. For the best results allow the wine to age for at least a year before drinking.

Here are some alternatives that can be used in the Denmark Wine recipe:

- Replace white sugar with brown sugar.
- Add 1 cup chopped almonds.
- Add ¾ cup onion and reduce the Brussels sprouts to 4 cups
- Replace the lemons with four oranges.
- If you want your wine to have a bolder taste, increase the raisins to 3 cups.

What's Up Doc Wine

Yield 1 Gallon/3.8 L

OG = 1.090 FG = 1.014 ABV = 10%

Ingredients:

- 3 ½ lbs carrots
- 1 lb raisins
- 5 cups granulated sugar
- ½ tsp yeast energizer
- 6 oranges, juice and rind
- ¼ tsp tannin
- 1 campden tablet
- 1 packet wine yeast
- Water
- Standard winemaking equipment
- 1-gallon carboy

Instructions:

1. Wash and scrub carrots and chop into small pieces. Put them into a pot and boil them until they are soft for about 15 to 20 minutes. Strain the liquid into primary fermenter. Do not press the carrot mash.

2. Add more water to carrot pieces and boil again for about five minutes. Strain into primary fermenter and again do not press the carrots. Discard the carrot mash. Add enough water to the liquid to make 1 gallon.

3. Cut up raisins and add to fermenter. Add the remaining ingredients except the yeast. Let sit 24 hours.

4. Be sure the SG is between 1.090 and 1.100. Pitch yeast. Stir the must for three or four days, until rapid fermentation ceases. Make sure you rack the wine in five days or the orange peel could leave a bitter taste in the wine.

5. Strain and rack into carboy. Attach airlock.

6. For a drier tasting wine, mature for at least three weeks, then rack and allow to mature four more weeks. The wine should be clear and the hydrometer readings stable before it is bottled.

7. For a sweeter tasting wine, mature for three weeks and then rack into another vessel. Dissolve ½ cup sugar in 1 cup of wine and pour the sweetened wine back into the fermentation vessel. Repeat this process until at least two hydrometer readings are stable, or every six weeks. Rack the wine every month until it is clear, then bottle.

8. Mature the wine for a year.

Amaizing Wine

Yield 1 Gallon/3.8 L

OG = 1.100 FG = 1.014 ABV = 12%

Ingredients:

- 12 cobs sweet corn*
- 4 cups corn syrup
- 2 oranges, juice only
- 1 teabag
- 1 tsp yeast energizer
- 1 campden tablet
- 1 packet wine yeast

- Water
- Standard winemaking equipment
- 1-gallon carboy

Instructions:

1. Cook corn on the cob and reserve the water to make the wine. Pour corn water into fermentation bucket. Add the remaining ingredients except the yeast. Let sit 24 hours.

2. Be sure the SG is between 1.090 and 1.100. Pitch yeast. Stir the must for three or four days, until rapid fermentation ceases.

3. Strain, rack into carboy, and attach airlock.

4. For a drier tasting wine, mature for at least three weeks, then rack and allow to mature four more weeks. The wine should be clear and the hydrometer readings stable before it is bottled.

5. For a sweet wine, rack at three weeks. Add ½ cup of sugar dissolved in 1 cup of wine. Stir gently, and place back into carboy. Repeat process every six weeks until specific gravity is stable. Rack every month until wine is clear. Bottle when the wine is ready.

*12 cobs of corn is just the minimum number needed to create this wine. If you use more cobs you will get a fuller flavor of your wine. If you find that you do not want to eat two dozen ears of corn, you can freeze the water until you have cooked enough to make the wine. If you find that you have more than a gallon of water, you can place the water on low heat and allow the liquid to concentrate.

Cuke Wine

Yield 1 Gallon/3.8 L

OG = 1.100 FG = 1.014 ABV = 12%

Ingredients:

- 4 lbs cucumbers*
- 3 campden tablets
- 2 oranges
- 2 lemons
- 7 cups sugar
- Pectic enzyme
- Yeast nutrients
- 1 packet wine yeast
- Water
- Standard winemaking equipment
- 1-gallon carboy
- Nylon bag/cheesecloth

Instructions:

1. Wash cucumbers. Chop cucumbers while leaving on the skin and put them in the bag. Wash oranges and lemons. Slice the fruit into thin pieces and add to cucumbers in the bag. Place bag in the primary fermenter. Add sugar and add the nutrients.

2. Pour a quart of boiling water over sugar to dissolve. After it cools, add pectic enzyme. Let sit for 24 hours.

3. Be sure the SG is between 1.090 and 1.100. Pitch yeast and stir for five days, until rapid fermentation ceases.

4. Remove the bag and gently squeeze. Rack into the carboy and attach airlock.

5. For a drier tasting wine, mature for at least three weeks, then rack and allow to mature four more weeks. The wine should be clear and the hydrometer readings stable before it is bottled.

6. For a sweet wine, rack at three weeks. Add ½ cup sugar dissolved in 1 cup wine. Stir gently, and place back into carboy. Repeat process every six weeks until specific gravity is stable. Rack every month until wine is clear. Bottle when the wine is ready.

Be aware that cucumbers have a high amount of water in them. You may want to watch how much water you add in the beginning of the process.

You can make an alternative version of the recipe by trying the following:

*   Replace the granulated sugar with honey or brown sugar.

*   You can spice up the wine by adding 1 ounce freshly sliced ginger root to the water before boiling it. Allow the mixture to simmer on low heat for about 15 minutes before adding to the cucumbers.

Sunchoke Wine

Yield 1 Gallon/3.8 L

OG = 1.100 FG = 1.014 ABV = 12%

Ingredients:

*   4 lbs Jerusalem Artichokes (also known as Sunchokes)
*   2 oranges, juiced
*   ½ tsp pectic enzyme
*   1 packet wine yeast
*   Water

- ½ lb raisins
- 6 cups granulated sugar
- ½ tsp yeast nutrient
- 2 campden tablets
- Standard winemaking equipment
- 1-gallon carboy

Instructions:

1. Clean the Jerusalem Artichokes and cut into slices. Add slices to a pot. Add 2 quarts of water and simmer on low until they are fork-tender.

2. Add the raisins, sugar, campden tablets, and nutrients into the fermentation bucket. Strain the Jerusalem Artichoke liquid into the fermentation bucket. Dissolve sugar into the must.

3. Take the used Jerusalem Artichokes and add them back into a pot. Add 2 quarts of water and boil them for another five minutes. Strain liquid into primary fermenter and throw out what is left of the Jerusalem Artichokes. Allow the must to cool and then add orange juice and pectic enzyme. Let sit for 24 hours.

4. Make sure the SG is between 1.090 and 1.100. Pitch yeast. Stir for five days or until rapid fermentation ceases.

5. Strain the liquid and rack it into a carboy. Attach airlock.

6. For a drier tasting wine, mature for at least three weeks, then rack and allow to mature four more weeks. The wine should be clear and the hydrometer readings stable before it is bottled.

7. For a sweet wine, rack at three weeks. Add ½ cup sugar dissolved in 1 cup wine. Stir gently, and place back into carboy. Repeat process every six weeks until specific gravity is stable. Rack every month until wine is clear. Bottle when the wine is ready.

Crybaby Wine

Yield 1 Gallon/3.8 L

OG = 1.100 FG = 1.014 ABV = 12%

Ingredients:

- ½ lb onions
- ½ lb potatoes
- 1 lb raisins
- 5 cups granulated sugar
- 1 tsp yeast nutrient
- 2 tsp acid blend
- 1 campden tablet
- 1 packet wine yeast
- Water
- Standard winemaking equipment
- 1-gallon carboy

Instructions:

1. Peel and wash peel onions. Cut up onions and potatoes. Boil them in 1 quart water for about 15 to 20 minutes. Strain the liquid from the potatoes and onions into fermentation bucket and discard the pulp. Bring the liquid to the 1-gallon mark.

2. Chop raisins and add to fermenter. Add the remaining ingredients except the yeast. Let sit 24 hours.

3. Make sure the SG is between 1.090 and 1.100. Pitch yeast. Stir must four days or until rapid fermentation ceases.

4. Strain and rack into carboy and attach airlock.

5. For a drier tasting wine, mature for at least three weeks, then rack and allow to mature four more weeks. The wine should be clear and the hydrometer readings stable before it is bottled.

6. For a sweet wine, rack at three weeks. Add ½ cup sugar dissolved in 1 cup wine. Stir gently, and place back into carboy. Repeat process every six weeks until specific gravity is stable. Rack every month until wine is clear. Bottle when the wine is ready.

7. Allow wine to mature for at least a year.

Snippy Wine

Yield 1 Gallon/3.8 L

OG = 1.100 FG = 1.014 ABV = 12%

Ingredients:

- 3 lbs parsnips
- 1 lb raisins
- 4 ½ cups granulated sugar
- ½ tsp yeast energizer
- 4 oranges, juice only
- ¼ tsp tannin
- 1 campden tablet
- 1 packet wine yeast
- Water
- Standard winemaking equipment
- 1-gallon carboy

Instructions:

1. Clean the parsnips and cut into slices. Add slices to a pot. Add 2 quarts of water and simmer on low until they are fork-tender.

2. Add the raisins, sugar, campden tablets, and nutrients into the fermentation bucket. Strain the parsnip liquid into the fermentation bucket. Dissolve sugar into the must.

3. Take the used parsnips and add them back into a pot. Add 2 quarts of water and boil them for another five minutes. Strain liquid into primary fermenter and throw out what is left of the parsnips. Allow the must to cool and then add orange juice and pectic enzyme. Let sit for 24 hours.

4. Make sure the SG is between 1.090 and 1.100. Pitch yeast. Stir for five days or until rapid fermentation ceases.

5. Strain the liquid and rack it into a carboy. Attach airlock.

6. For a drier tasting wine, mature for at least three weeks, then rack and allow to mature four more weeks. The wine should be clear and the hydrometer readings stable before it is bottled.

7. For a sweet wine, rack at three weeks. Add ½ cup sugar dissolved in 1 cup wine. Stir gently, and place back into carboy. Repeat process every six weeks until specific gravity is stable. Rack every month until wine is clear. Bottle when the wine is ready.

Two Peas in a Pod Wine

Yield 1 Gallon/ 3.8 L

OG = 1.100 FG = 1.014 ABV = 12%

Ingredients:

- 5 lbs pea pods
- 6 ½ cups granulated sugar
- 1 tsp yeast nutrients
- 2 tsp acid blend
- ½ tsp pectic enzyme
- 1 campden tablet

- Juice of 4 oranges
- Water
- 1 packet wine yeast
- Standard winemaking equipment
- 1-gallon carboy

Instructions:

1. Clean the pea pods and cut into slices. Add slices to a pot. Add 2 quarts of water and simmer on low until they are fork tender.

2. Add the raisins, sugar, campden tablets, and nutrients into the fermentation bucket. Strain the pea pods liquid into the fermentation bucket. Dissolve sugar into the must.

3. Take the used pea pods and add them back into a pot. Add 2 quarts of water and boil them for another five minutes. Strain liquid into primary fermenter and throw out what is left of the pea pods. Allow the must to cool and then add orange juice and pectic enzyme. Let sit for 24 hours.

4. Make sure the SG is between 1.090 and 1.100. Pitch yeast. Stir for five days or until rapid fermentation ceases.

5. Strain the liquid and rack it into a carboy. Attach airlock.

6. For a drier tasting wine, mature for at least three weeks, then rack and allow to mature four more weeks. The wine should be clear and the hydrometer readings stable before it is bottled.

7. For a sweet wine, rack at three weeks. Add ½ cup sugar dissolved in 1 cup wine. Stir gently, and place back into carboy. Repeat process every six weeks until specific gravity is stable. Rack every month until wine is clear. Bottle when the wine is ready.

The Great Pumpkin Wine

Yield 1 Gallon/3.8 L

OG = 1.090 FG = 1.014 ABV = 10%

Ingredients:

- 8 cups pumpkin (Do not use canned pumpkin)
- 5 cups sugar
- 1 tsp yeast nutrient
- 3 tsp acid blend
- 1 campden tablet
- 1 lb raisins
- 1 packet wine yeast
- Water
- Standard winemaking equipment
- 1-gallon carboy
- Nylon bag/cheesecloth

Instructions:

1. Wash, trim, peel, chop, and mash the pumpkin. Place pumpkin in the bag/cloth. Add raisins to bag and place in the primary fermenter. Place bag in primary fermenter and add boiling water. Let sit 24 hours.

2. Add remaining ingredients except yeast. Dissolve sugar into the must. Be sure the SG is between 1.090 and 1.095. Pitch yeast and stir. Stir five days or until the SG 1.040.

3. Remove the bag and squeeze out the liquid. Rack the liquid into the carboy. Add water to make 1 gallon and attach airlock.

4. For a drier tasting wine, mature for at least three weeks, then rack and allow to mature four more weeks. The wine should be clear and the hydrometer readings stable before it is bottled.

5. For a sweeter tasting wine, mature for three weeks and then rack into another vessel. Dissolve ½ cup sugar in 1 cup of wine and pour the sweetened wine back into the fermentation vessel. Repeat this process until at least two hydrometer readings are stable, or every six weeks. Rack the wine every month until it is clear, then bottle.

6. For the best results allow the wine to age for at least a year before drinking.

You can add different ingredients to the pumpkin wine for a variety of different flavors and results.

Addition No. 1:

- 1 cinnamon stick
- 1 inch-long fresh ginger root
- 1 whole stick of nutmeg

Addition No. 2:

- 1 4-inch cinnamon stick
- 1 1-inch fresh ginger root
- 1 whole stick of nutmeg
- 1 tsp whole cloves

Addition No. 3:

- 1 4-inch cinnamon stick
- 1 whole stick of nutmeg
- 2 tsp whole cardamom seeds

You should add spices to the water before boiling. You can also replace granulated sugar with light brown sugar.

Sweet Tater Wine

Yield 1 Gallon/3.8 L

OG = 1.090 FG = 1.014 ABV = 10%

Ingredients:

- 12 cups chopped sweet potatoes or yams
- 5 ½ cups granulated sugar
- 2 cups light raisins
- 1 tsp yeast nutrients
- 2 oranges
- ½ tsp pectic enzyme
- 1 campden tablet
- Water
- 1 packet wine yeast
- Standard winemaking equipment
- 1-gallon carboy
- Nylon bag/cheesecloth

Instructions:

1. Peel and cube sweet potatoes. Place sweet potato in a large pot of boiling water. Simmer the potatoes for 25 minutes. Chop raisins and place them into fermentation bucket. Strain liquid from the potatoes into primary fermenter and squeeze out all liquid from the pulp. You can use the potatoes for another dish to eat if you wish. Bring the level of the must to 1 gallon by adding water. Slice oranges thinly and place in bag/cloth. Add remaining ingredients except the yeast. Stir to dissolve sugar. Let sit 24 hours.

2. The specific gravity should be between 1.090 and 1.100. Stir in yeast. Stir for five days or until rapid fermentation ceases. Remove bag and rack into carboy. Attach airlock.

3. For a drier wine, mature for three weeks, then rack and allow to mature another four weeks. When the wine is clear and no longer needs racking, then it is ready to bottle.

4. For a sweet wine, rack at three weeks. Add ½ cup sugar dissolved in 1 cup wine. Stir gently, and place back into carboy. Repeat process every six weeks until specific gravity is stable. Rack every month until wine is clear. Bottle when the wine is ready.

5. For the best results, allow the wine to mature for are least one year from the date it was started before you drink it.

The question of whether a tomato is a fruit or vegetable is a topic of hot debate among my daughters. Technically, a tomato is a fruit. A tomato is developed from the ovary in the base of the flower and contains the seeds of the plant. There are even exceptions, as some cultivars do not have seeds in the fruit. This topic is not just debated at my particular dinner table, but hotly debated between scientists and chefs worldwide. This next wine is my homage to this old debate. I chose to place it under vegetables because it is usually used in the culinary world as a vegetable. Tomato ice cream does not sound too appetizing. However, tomato wine is delicious.

Is it Fruit or Vegetable Wine

Yield 1 Gallon/ 3.8 L

OG = 1.090 FG = 1.014 ABV = 10%

Ingredients:

- 5 lbs ripe tomatoes
- 4 cups granulated sugar
- 1 tsp yeast nutrient
- 2 lemons, juice only
- 2 campden tablets
- ½ tsp pectic enzyme
- 1 packet wine yeast
- Water
- Standard winemaking equipment
- 1-gallon carboy
- Nylon bag/cheesecloth

Instructions:

1. Wash and remove vine from tomatoes. Chop and place bag/cloth into the primary fermenter. Make sure that the must level is at 1 gallon by adding water. Add remaining ingredients except yeast. Stir well to dissolve sugar. Let sit 24 hours.

2. Make sure the SG is between 1.090 and 1.095. Pitch yeast and stir. Stir for five days or until specific gravity is 1.040.

3. Remove bag and gently squeeze out as much juice as you can from the fruit. Rack into carboy and attach airlock.

4. For a drier tasting wine, mature for at least three weeks, then rack and allow to mature four more weeks. The wine should be clear and the hydrometer readings stable before it is bottled.

5. For a sweet wine, rack at three weeks. Add ½ cup sugar dissolved in 1 cup wine. Stir gently, and place back into carboy. Repeat process every six weeks until specific gravity is stable. Rack every month until wine is clear. Bottle when the wine is ready.

One variation on this tomato wine recipe is to place tomatoes in a saucepan and cover with water. Boil tomatoes until they are soft and then mash. Add mash to nylon bag/cheesecloth and place in fermenter. Make sure the must is at the gallon mark by adding water. Add remaining ingredients except yeast. Allow sitting 24 hours, and then pitching the yeast. Stir daily for three days. Rack into carboy. Attach airlock. Finish as a dry or sweet wine mentioned in the original recipe.

Fried green tomatoes are one of my favorite southern dishes. It is simple to make. Slice a green tomato, dip in egg wash, flour, egg wash again, and crushed corn flakes. Quickly place it in a frying pan with vegetable oil heated to 350 degrees. Allow it to fry for three minutes and then flip it. Allow it to cook for a further three minutes. Serve hot with some horseradish sauce. To wash it down, try creating this wine at home.

Non-Fried Green Tomato Wine

Yield 1 Gallon/3.8 L

OG = 1.100 FG = 1.014 ABV = 12%

Ingredients:

- 3 ½ lbs green tomatoes
- 5 cups granulated sugar
- 1 tsp yeast nutrient
- 4 lemons, juice only
- 1 campden tablet
- ½ tsp pectic enzyme
- 2 lbs raisins
- ½ oz fresh ginger root (optional)
- 1 packet wine yeast
- Water
- Standard winemaking equipment
- 1-gallon carboy
- Nylon bag/cheesecloth

Instructions:

1. Wash and remove vine from tomatoes. Chop and place bag/cloth into the primary fermenter. Make sure that the must level is at 1 gallon by adding water. Add remaining ingredients except yeast. Stir well to dissolve sugar. Let sit 24 hours.

2. Make sure the SG is between 1.090 and 1.095. Pitch yeast and stir. Stir for five days or until specific gravity is 1.040.

3. Remove bag and gently squeeze out as much juice as you can from the fruit. Rack into carboy and attach airlock.

4. For a drier tasting wine, mature for at least three weeks, then rack and allow to mature four more weeks. The wine should be clear and the hydrometer readings stable before it is bottled.

5. For a sweeter tasting wine, mature for three weeks and then rack into another vessel. Dissolve ½ cup sugar in 1 cup of wine and pour the sweetened wine back into the fermentation vessel. Repeat this process until at least two hydrometer readings are stable, or every six weeks. Rack the wine every month until it is clear, then bottle.

Virtual 8 Wine

Yield 1 Gallon/ 3.8 L

OG = 1.090 FG = 1.014 ABV = 10%

Ingredients:

- Juice from 18 lb (8.2 kg) tomatoes (about 1.67 gallons (6.3 liters))
- 5 lbs cane sugar
- Water
- 8 tsp tartaric acid
- 1 tsp (2.3 g) pectic enzyme
- 2 campden tablets
- Premier cuvee yeast
- 1-gallon carboy
- Standard winemaking equipment

Instructions:

1. Parboil the tomatoes and remove the skin. Remove the seeds from the tomatoes and juice the rest in a food processor. Pour the juice into the fermenter. Dissolve the sugar in the boiling water. Allow the water to cool and add to fermenter. Add sulfite, pectic enzyme, and tartaric acid. Pitch the yeast.

2. Make sure the SG is between 1.090 and 1.095. Pitch yeast and stir. Stir for five days or until specific gravity is 1.040.

3. Remove bag and gently squeeze out as much juice as you can from the fruit. Rack into carboy and attach airlock.

4. For a drier tasting wine, mature for at least three weeks, then rack and allow to mature four more weeks. The wine should be clear and the hydrometer readings stable before it is bottled.

5. For a sweeter tasting wine, mature for three weeks and then rack into another vessel. Dissolve ½ cup sugar in 1 cup of wine and pour the sweetened wine back into the fermentation vessel. Repeat this process until at least two hydrometer readings are stable, or every six weeks. Rack the wine every month until it is clear, then bottle.

Chilled Chile Wine

Yield 1 Gallon/3.8 L

OG = 1.055 FG = 1.014 ABV = 7%

Ingredients:

- 2 lbs New Mexico green chilies roasted, frozen, thawed, and peeled
- Zest of two lemons
- 5 lb bag of white sugar
- 1 tbsp yeast nutrients
- 1-gallon carboy
- Nylon bag or cheesecloth
- Standard winemaking equipment

Instructions:

1. Place chile and lemon zest in cheesecloth. Place in 3 quarts of water and boil for 20 minutes. Place water and cheesecloth in fermenter overnight.

2. Dissolve sugar into must by stirring. Pitch yeast and nutrients in the fermenter and bring up to 1 gallon. Allow to ferment until rapid fermentation ceases. Remove bag and gently squeeze. Rack into carboy and attach airlock.

3. For a drier tasting wine, mature for at least three weeks, then rack and allow to mature four more weeks. The wine should be clear and the hydrometer readings stable before it is bottled.

4. For a sweeter tasting wine, mature for three weeks and then rack into another vessel. Dissolve ½ cup sugar in 1 cup of wine and pour the sweetened wine back into the fermentation vessel. Repeat this process until at least two hydrometer readings are stable, or every six weeks. Rack the wine every month until it is clear, then bottle.

Beanie Zucchini Wine

Yield 1 Gallon/3.8 L

OG = 1.100 FG = 1.014 ABV = 12%

Ingredients:

- 4 lbs zucchini
- 3 campden tablets
- 2 oranges
- 2 lemons
- 7 cups sugar
- Yeast nutrients
- 1 packet wine yeast
- Pectic enzyme
- Standard winemaking equipment
- 1-gallon carboy

- Water
- Nylon bag/cheesecloth

Instructions:

1. Wash zucchini and chop. Leave the skin on the zucchini Place the pieces in the bag/cloth. Wash oranges and lemons and slice thinly. Add fruit to the bag with zucchini. Add bag to primary fermenter. Stir in sugar and nutrients. Pour 16 cups boiling water over mixture. Stir to dissolve sugar. Let cool and then add pectic enzyme. Let sit for 24 hours.

2. Be sure the SG is between 1.090 and 1.100. Pitch yeast. Stir daily for five days until rapid fermentation ceases.

3. Remove bag and squeeze out liquid gently. Rack liquid to the carboy and attach airlock.

4. For a drier tasting wine, mature for at least three weeks, then rack and allow to mature four more weeks. The wine should be clear and the hydrometer readings stable before it is bottled.

5. For a sweeter tasting wine, mature for three weeks and then rack into another vessel. Dissolve ½ cup sugar in 1 cup of wine and pour the sweetened wine back into the fermentation vessel. Repeat this process until at least two hydrometer readings are stable, or every six weeks. Rack the wine every month until it is clear, then bottle.

> To spice up your zucchini wine, replace granulated sugar with honey or brown sugar. You can also add 1 oz fresh, thinly sliced ginger root and boil. Let must simmer on low for about 15 minutes before pouring it over the cucumbers.

CHAPTER 5

Grain Wines

The creation of the Château Jiahu was similar to the process that was used in recreating the Midas Touch brew (see appendix). Pottery fragments were discovered in the 9,000-year-old Jiahu ruins in China's Henan Province. The ruins had been covered by a flood and were rediscovered in the 1980s.

In 2004, American archeologist professor Patrick McGovern discovered alcohol traces in the pottery fragments. His laboratory analysis found honey, Chinese hawthorn, grapes, rice, and other ingredients. This discovery made China the earliest country that brewed wine.

Dogfish Head Brewery soon after recreated this ancient brew, called Château Jiahu. The brew is about 8 percent alcohol and is the color of golden champagne. The brewery tested it with a small group and after a positive response, decided to commercially produce it.

Ancient Chinese Secret

Yield 5 gallons/19 L

OG = 1.088 FG = 1.014 ABV = 10%

Ingredients:

- 2 lbs two-row pale malt
- 2 lbs 2 oz. Munton's light dried malt extract
- 4 lbs Munton's light liquid malt extract
- 3 lbs orange blossom honey
- 2 lbs rice syrup
- 1 lb Alexander's Muscat grape concentrate
- 1 can frozen grape juice concentrate (100 percent fruit, no added sugar)
- ½ lb Hawthorn berry powder
- ¼ oz. Simcoe hops
- Sake yeast
- Standard winemaking supplies
- Nylon steeping bag/cheesecloth

Instructions:

1. If malt is not crushed, you can place it in the cheesecloth and use a rolling pin and crush the grains. A hand grinder will work nicely.

2. Place crushed grains in a nylon bag/cloth and steep 2.5 quarts/2.4 liters of water at 149 degrees F/65 degrees C for 45 minutes.

3. Bring 2 gallons of water to a boil in a separate brew pot while grains are steeping.

4. After steeping the grains place bag in a colander over brew pot. Pour the liquid from the steeping pot through the bag.

5. Rinse grain bag with 1.5 quarts of 170 degrees F/77 degrees C water into the brew pot.

6. Bring this must to a boil and then add dried malt extract.

7. Allow the must to boil 15 minutes.

8. Add hops and allow must to boil for another 60 minutes.

9. Dissolve liquid malt extract in the must and allow a final 15 minutes of boiling.

10. Remove pot from the heat and stir in honey and hawthorn berry powder.

11. Allow the brew to cool, and then transfer to the fermentation bucket.

12. Bring fermenter volume to 5 gallons with water. Pitch the sake yeast.

13. Place fermenter in a dark place and cover with lid and add fermentation lock.

14. Watch the daily and when rapid fermentation ceases, add Muscat grape juice and frozen grape juice concentrate. After 12 to 14 days, place in a cool place and cold condition for 21 days. Bottle when wine is ready.

15. Mature wine for a year from the beginning of the process.

Demeter and Persephone Wine

Yield 1 Gallon/ 3.8 L

OG = 1.04 FG = 1.014 ABV = 10%

Ingredients:

- 8 pomegranates*
- 1 lb raisins
- 1 cup dry malt extract
- 4 ½ cups granulated sugar
- 2 tsp acid blend
- 1 tsp pectic enzyme
- 1 tsp yeast nutrient
- 1 campden tablet
- 1 packet wine yeast
- Water
- 1-gallon carboy
- Standard winemaking equipment
- Nylon bag/cheesecloth

Instructions:

1. Cut open pomegranates. Put seeds in bag/cloth. Do not get any pith or skin. Be careful as the fruit is around the outside seeds, so it is a good idea to do this over the fermenter so you will not lose any juice. Crush the fruit and place bag in fermenter. Pour boiling water into fermenter. Add sugar, stirring to dissolve. Let sit 24 hours.

2. Be sure the SG is between 1.090 and 1.100. Slice the whole lemon, rind and all, and add to primary. Add the remaining ingredients, including the yeast. Stir daily for five days as fermentation begins.

3. Remove bag and gently squeeze. Rack into secondary fermenter and attach airlock.

4. For a drier tasting wine, mature for at least three weeks, then rack and allow to mature four more weeks. The wine should be clear and the hydrometer readings stable before it is bottled.

5. To create a sweeter tasting wine, mature for three weeks, then rack wine into another vessel. Dissolve ½ cup sugar in 1 cup wine and pour the sweetened wine into the fermentation vessel. Repeat this process every six weeks or when at least two hydrometer readings are stable. Rack the wine every month until the wine is clear, then bottle.

6. For the best results allow the wine to age for at least a year before drinking.

Pomegranates can be found in different sizes. Be aware that using eight large fruit you will have a fuller-bodied wine, but using smaller fruit will not take as long to age.

As the Greek myth goes, the goddess Persephone went to the underworld to be with Hades. She did not want to stay there, but after she descended she ate pomegranate and sealed her fate: she was to stay in the underworld forever. Her mother, the goddess Demeter, searched the earth for Persephone. As the goddess of the grain, the world was thrown into winter as Demeter mourned for her missing daughter. Now, Persephone spends half the year with her mother (spring and summer) and must descend to the underworld the other half to be with her consort, Hades (fall and winter).

Sow Your Wild Oats

Yield 1 Gallon/ 3.8 L

OG = 1.04 FG = 1.014 ABV = 10%

Ingredients:

- 6 cups wild oats
- Water
- 9 cups sugar
- 2 oranges
- 2 lemons
- Wine yeast
- 1-gallon carboy
- Nylon bag/cheesecloth
- Standard winemaking equipment

Instructions:

1. Clean oats. Place oats in cheesecloth/bag. Squeeze juice from lemon and orange into fermenter. Place the peel and rind in the cheesecloth. Simmer the oats on low for 20 minutes in 3 quarts of water. Squeeze out all of the liquid into the primary fermenter. Discard pulp. Raise the level of the must to 1 gallon by adding water. Add sugar and raisins. Stir the must in order to dissolve sugar. Let sit 24 hours.

2. Make sure the SG is between 1.090 and 1.100. Pitch yeast. Stir for three days or until rapid fermentation ceases. Rack into carboy and attach airlock.

3. For a drier tasting wine, mature for at least three weeks, then rack and allow to mature four more weeks. The wine should be clear and the hydrometer readings stable before it is bottled.

4. For a sweeter tasting wine, mature for three weeks and then rack into another vessel. Dissolve ½ cup sugar in 1 cup of wine and pour the sweetened wine back into the fermentation vessel. Repeat this process until at least two hydrometer readings are stable, or every six weeks. Rack the wine every month until it is clear, then bottle.

5. For the best results, allow the wine to mature for are least one year from the date it was started before you drink it.

> Rice wine is not the same as sake. Sake uses a totally different process, which includes inoculating rice with a mold before fermentation.

Rice Patty Wine

Yield 1 Gallon/3.8 L

OG = 1.04 FG = 1.014 ABV = 10%

Ingredients:

- 4 cups raw wild rice
- 7 cups of sugar
- 1 ½ cups raisins
- Wine yeast
- Water
- 1-gallon carboy
- Standard winemaking equipment
- Nylon bag/cheesecloth

Instructions:

1. Clean rice in running water. Place rice and raisins in cheesecloth/ bag. Simmer the rice on low for 20 minutes in 3 quarts of water. Place liquid and bag in primary fermenter. Raise the level of the must to 1 gallon by adding water. Add sugar and raisins. Stir the must in order to dissolve sugar. Let sit 24 hours.

2. Make sure the SG is between 1.090 and1.100. Pitch yeast. Stir for three days or until rapid fermentation ceases. Remove bag and squeeze out the liquid. Rack into carboy and attach airlock.

3. For a drier tasting wine, mature for at least three weeks, then rack and allow to mature four more weeks. The wine should be clear and the hydrometer readings stable before it is bottled.

4. For a sweeter tasting wine, mature for three weeks and then rack into another vessel. Dissolve ½ cup sugar in 1 cup of wine and pour the sweetened wine back into the fermentation vessel. Repeat this process until at least two hydrometer readings are stable, or every six weeks. Rack the wine every month until it is clear, then bottle.

5. For the best results, allow the wine to mature for are least one year from the date it was started before you drink it.

CHAPTER 6

Herbal Wines

There are a number of distilled liquors made from herbs. They are chosen for the flavors they can add to a drink such as mint, licorice, or bitter flavors. Herbal wines contain herbs for the same reason. Most herbs do not contain enough residual sugar to ferment and therefore require added sugar.

The trick with herbs is to know how to draw the volatile oils from them in order to experience their unique tastes. In this section I have separated the wines according to the part of the plant that is used in creating flavors of these unique wild wines.

Before you proceed there are a few words of warning I would like to impart. Unless you know what you are doing, it is not recommended that you pick strange plants and herbs and try to make a wine out of them. Some herbs are poisonous, and there are even plants that look like a particular plant but are in fact totally different.

If you do choose to pick herbs to create wild wines from, you should not pick them in populated areas such as roadsides. The exhaust they filter every day can taint these herbs. You should instead find a meadow away from populated areas. Be sure you are not picking plants in a national park, because there are laws against this activity.

The best way to be sure you are using the right herb and that it was picked legally is to grow it yourself. Many herbs can be grown in pots or in a simple plot next to your house. Make sure that you do not use a lot of pesticides on your herbs, or any other plant you are using to create wine from. If you did use some sort of herbicide or pesticide, wash the plants thoroughly before using. There are many different techniques of organic farming that can be utilized that would reduce your need to use poisonous chemicals. You can look for books online, at your local library, or contact your local agricultural extension office for details.

The second best way to obtain herbs is to look at local farmers markets. They will often have vendors that sell different types of fresh and potted herbs. Make sure you are using fresh herbs and not dried herbs. Each of these recipes requires use of fresh herbs, and the use of dried herbs can have mixed results. They would have to be used in different amounts, and sometimes dried herbs are treated with chemicals to preserve them. These preservatives can ruin your wine.

Roots

The roots of herbs are often hard and take extra work to extract the volatile oils from. You often have to boil them for a longer amount of time and some require that your break up the flesh and macerate the herb. Many of the root wines will have an underlying earthy flavor to them. This can be strong or subtle depending on the type of wine you are creating.

It is important that you scrub and sometimes peel roots as dirt and debris can be stuck to them because they are growing underground. You do not want dirt in your wine. It would probably sink to the bottom but it can impart flavors in your wine.

Anise is a strong flavored herb and it is described as have a licorice flavor. Often the seeds are used in confections such as Norwegian knots, Italian pizzelle, Netherland Muisjes, Peruvian Picarones, Mexican atole de anis, and as Australian Humbugs, British Aniseed balls, New Zealand Aniseed wheels, German pfeffernusse, and springerle champurrado, which is a Mexican hot chocolate drink.

Anise is also used in liquors such as the Greek Ouzo, Absinthe, Anisette, the German Jägermeister, Pastis, the Arabic Arak, the Colombian national drink Aguardiente, the Turkish Raki and there is some speculation that it is used in the French liqueur Chartreuse. Virgil's Root Beer in the United Sated also uses anise as an ingredient in their root beer. This recipe is slightly different in that it uses the root, which has a milder licorice flavor.

Anise Foot Wine

Yield 1 Gallon/3.8 L

OG = 1.090 FG = 1.014 ABV = 10%

Ingredients:

- 4 cups of anise root (fresh or dried)
- Water
- 6 cups of sugar
- 3 cups of raisins
- 1 orange
- 1 lemon
- Wine yeast
- 1-gallon carboy
- Standard winemaking equipment

Instructions:

1. Clean dirt from anise root. Scrub it well and slice it. Place root in cheesecloth/bag. Squeeze juice from lemon and orange into fermenter. Place the peel and rind in the cheesecloth. Simmer the anise root on low for 20 minutes in 3 quarts of water. Squeeze out all of the liquid into the primary fermenter. Discard pulp. Raise the level of the must to 1 gallon by adding water. Add sugar and raisins. Stir the must in order to dissolve sugar. Let sit 24 hours.

2. Make sure the SG is between 1.090 and 1.100. Pitch yeast. Stir for three days or until rapid fermentation ceases. Rack into carboy and attach airlock.

3. For a drier tasting wine, mature for at least three weeks, then rack and allow to mature four more weeks. The wine should be clear and the hydrometer readings stable before it is bottled.

4. For a sweeter tasting wine, mature for three weeks and then rack into another vessel. Dissolve ½-cup sugar in 1 cup of wine and pour the sweetened wine back into the fermentation vessel. Repeat this process until at least two hydrometer readings are stable, or every six weeks. Rack the wine every month until it is clear, then bottle.

5. For the best results, allow the wine to mature for at least one year from the date it was started before you drink it.

Coltsfoot is a common herb that is often used in folk remedies to treat asthma and bronchitis. This herb can be picked in the early spring when it has a flat orange flower head. When picked early, the plant is sweet. If you wait too long it can taste bitter.

Pony Up Wine

Yield 1 Gallon/3.8 L

OG = 1.090 FG = 1.014 ABV = 10%

Ingredients:

- 4 cups of sliced coltsfoot
- Water
- 8 cups sugar
- 1 lemon
- 1 orange
- Wine yeast
- 1-gallon carboy
- Standard winemaking equipment
- Nylon bag/cheesecloth

Instructions:

1. Mash the coltsfoot in bucket of cold water. Remove dirt and debris from the root. Scrub the root and then slice it. Place root in cheesecloth/bag. Squeeze juice from lemon and orange into fermenter. Place the peel and rind in the cheesecloth. Simmer the root on low for 20 minutes in 3 quarts of water. Squeeze out all of the liquid into the primary fermenter. Discard pulp. Raise the level of the must to 1 gallon by adding water. Add sugar and raisins. Stir the must in order to dissolve sugar. Let sit 24 hours.

2. Make sure the SG is between 1.090 and 1.100. Pitch yeast. Stir for three days or until rapid fermentation ceases. Rack into carboy and attach airlock.

3. For a drier tasting wine, mature for at least three weeks, then rack and allow to mature four more weeks. The wine should be clear and the hydrometer readings stable before it is bottled.

4. For a sweeter tasting wine, mature for three weeks and then rack into another vessel. Dissolve ½ cup sugar in 1 cup of wine and pour

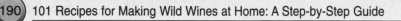

the sweetened wine back into the fermentation vessel. Repeat this process until at least two hydrometer readings are stable, or every six weeks. Rack the wine every month until it is clear, then bottle.

5. For the best results, allow the wine to mature for at least one year from the date it was started before you drink it.

Burdock is a medicinal herb that is thought of mostly as a weed. It grows very large leaves and is in the thistle family. It grows bristly seedpods that can attach themselves to clothing. The root has been used for centuries as a blood purifier. You need to dig deep to get this root because it is large and holds on fast.

Take Me With You Wine

Yield 1 Gallon/3.8 L

OG = 1.090 FG = 1.014 ABV = 10%

Ingredients:

- ½ lb of 2nd-year green burdock leaves and burrs and root
- 4 lbs brown sugar
- Standard winemaking equipment
- 1 large or 2 small lemons (juice only)
- 1 tsp yeast nutrient
- 1 crushed campden tablet
- 1 packet Tokay wine yeast
- Water
- 1-gallon carboy
- Nylon cloth/cheesecloth

Instructions:

1. Place leaves, burrs, and root into a bucket. Scrub and slice the root and wash the burrs and leaves. Add burdock and brown sugar place in the bag/cheesecloth. Place bag in the primary fermenter.

2. Squeeze all the juice from the lemon and add it to boiling water. Stir and dissolve sugar in the water. Pour the boiling water over the burdock in the fermenter. Add remaining ingredients except the yeast. Cover primary fermenter and allow to sit 24 hours.

3. Pitch yeast. After five days of rapid fermentation, remove bag and gently squeeze out the juice.

4. For a drier tasting wine, mature for at least three weeks, then rack and allow to mature four more weeks. The wine should be clear and the hydrometer readings stable before it is bottled.

5. For a sweeter tasting wine, mature for three weeks and then rack into another vessel. Dissolve ½ cup sugar in 1 cup of wine and pour the sweetened wine back into the fermentation vessel. Repeat this process until at least two hydrometer readings are stable, or every six weeks. Rack the wine every month until it is clear, then bottle.

6. For the best results, allow the wine to mature for at least one year from the date it was started before you drink it.

Leaf and Stem

Using the leaf and stem of herbs are slightly easier to work with than the roots. You need to only crush and boil them to remove the volatile oils you will need to flavor your wine. Make sure you use green leaves. If the plant has gone to seed, then the leaves can be bitter. You can extend the sweetness of your herbs leaves by pinching off flower heads that form.

Original Oregano Wine

Yield 1 Gallon/3.8 L

OG = 1.110 FG = 1.014 ABV = 15%

Ingredients:

- 4 to 6 cups of lightly packed fresh oregano (do not used dried)
- Water
- 3 lbs cane sugar or 3 ½ lbs honey
- 1 tsp yeast nutrient
- Standard winemaking equipment
- 1 tsp tannin
- 3 tsp acid blend
- 1 campden tablet
- Wine yeast
- 1-gallon carboy

Instructions:

1. Remove any dead leaves, bugs, and debris from the oregano. Rinse the oregano in cold water and then place in a 2-quart saucepan with 1 quart of water. Bring oregano to a simmer. As soon as it start simmering, take it off the heat and let sit for one to two hours.

2. Dissolve the sugar in boiling water. Strain the oregano and infused water to the sugar water. Dissolve the tannin, yeast nutrient, campden tablet, and 1 tsp of the acid. Pour mixture into the fermenter. Allow to sit overnight.

3. Take a hydrometer reading. It should be around 1.110. Pitch the yeast.

4. For a drier tasting wine, mature for at least three weeks, then rack and allow to mature four more weeks. The wine should be clear and the hydrometer readings stable before it is bottled.

5. For a sweeter tasting wine, mature for three weeks and then rack into another vessel. Dissolve ½ cup sugar in 1 cup of wine and pour

the sweetened wine back into the fermentation vessel. Repeat this process until at least two hydrometer readings are stable, or every six weeks. Rack the wine every month until it is clear, then bottle.

6. For the best results, allow the wine to mature for at least one year from the date it was started before you drink it.

For this recipe it is best to use broad leaf Italian parsley, rather than many other hybrids you might find at the local plant nursery.

Scarborough Faire Wine

Yield 1 Gallon/ 3.8 L

OG = 1.090 FG = 1.014 ABV = 10%

Ingredients:

- 1 quart fresh parsley (do not use dried parsley)
- 2 oranges
- 7 cups of sugar
- 2 tbsp lemon juice
- 3 cloves
- 1 campden tablet
- Standard winemaking equipment
- 1 packet wine yeast
- 1 tsp yeast nutrient
- 1 ½ cups orange juice (unsweetened)
- 1 tsp pcctic enzyme
- 1-gallon carboy
- Nylon bag/cheesecloth

Instructions:

1. Place parsley in a bucket with cold water. Remove dirt and debris from the root. Place parsley in cheesecloth/bag. Squeeze juice from lemon and orange into fermenter. Place the peel and rind in the cheesecloth. Simmer the root on low for 20 minutes in 3 quarts of water. Squeeze out all of the liquid into the primary fermenter. Discard pulp. Raise the level of the must to 1 gallon by adding wa-

ter. Add sugar and cloves. Stir the must in order to dissolve sugar. Let sit 24 hours.

2. Make sure the SG is between 1.090 and 1.100. Add yeast nutrient. Pitch yeast. Stir for three days or until rapid fermentation ceases. Rack into carboy and attach airlock.

3. For a drier tasting wine, mature for at least three weeks, then rack and allow to mature four more weeks. The wine should be clear and the hydrometer readings stable before it is bottled.

4. For a sweeter tasting wine, mature for three weeks and then rack into another vessel. Dissolve ½-cup sugar in 1 cup of wine and pour the sweetened wine back into the fermentation vessel. Repeat this process until at least two hydrometer readings are stable, or every six weeks. Rack the wine every month until it is clear, then bottle.

5. For the best results, allow the wine to mature for at least one year from the date it was started before you drink it.

Flowers

Like leaves and stems, flowers are simple to work with. The difference is flowers do not last very long, so you will have to look carefully and often to notice when flowers have bloomed. Once they are past their prime, they do not work well as a wine, so you need to pick them just after they have bloomed. Most flower wines are sweet and aromatic.

Hawthorn Flower Wine

Yield 1 Gallon/3.8 L

OG = 1.100 FG = 1.014 ABV = 12%

Ingredients:

- 3 quarts Hawthorn flowers
- Water
- 6 cups sugar
- 3 cups raisins
- Packet wine yeast
- 1-gallon carboy
- Nylon bag/cheesecloth
- Standard winemaking equipment

Instructions:

1. Remove any dead leaves, bugs, and debris from the flowers. Rinse the flowers in cold water and then place in a 2-quart (same as a 2-liter) saucepan with 1 quart of water. Bring flowers to a simmer. As soon as it start simmering, take it off the heat and let sit for one to two hours.

2. Dissolve the sugar in boiling water. Strain the hawthorn flowers and infused water to the sugar water. Add raisins. Pour mixture into the fermenter. Allow to sit overnight.

3. Take a hydrometer reading. It should be around 1.110. Pitch the yeast.

4. For a drier tasting wine, mature for at least three weeks, then rack and allow to mature four more weeks. The wine should be clear and the hydrometer readings stable before it is bottled.

5. For a sweeter tasting wine, mature for three weeks and then rack into another vessel. Dissolve ½ cup sugar in 1 cup of wine and pour the sweetened wine back into the fermentation vessel. Repeat this process until at least two hydrometer readings are stable, or every six weeks. Rack the wine every month until it is clear, then bottle.

6. For the best results, allow the wine to mature for at least one year from the date it was started before you drink it.

Lucky Clover Wine

Make sure you use the purple clover blossoms rather than the white. The purple ones are much sweeter. I remember finding these as a child and eating the clover heads because they were so sweet.

Yield 1 Gallon/3.8 L

OG = 1.100 FG = 1.014 ABV = 12%

Ingredients:

- 1 cup honey
- 6 cups sugar
- 3 lemons
- 2 oranges
- 2 tbsp acid blend
- 1 gallon purple clover blossoms (lightly packed)
- 1 tsp nutrients
- 3 campden tablets
- 1 packet wine yeast
- Water
- Standard winemaking equipment
- 1-gallon carboy
- Nylon bag/cheesecloth

Instructions:

1. Boil the honey in 4 cups water in a large pot. Skim off the foam that will form. Continue to boil until there is no longer any foam.

2. Dissolve sugar and with a quart of water and bring to a boil. Add nutrients and campden tablets. Remove from mixture from the heat.

3. Add clover flowers, fruit juices, and grated rinds into a bag/cloth. Place bag in primary fermenter. Pour boiled sugar mixture over the bag and allow it to sit for 24 hours.

4. Specific gravity should be 1.100. Add yeast. Stir daily for five days.

5. Remove bag and rack liquid to the carboy. Attach an airlock. Rack when fermentation ceases, which will take about six weeks.

6. For a dry wine, rack in three weeks, and again in four weeks. Continue racking every month until wine is clear. Bottle when the wine is ready.

7. For a sweeter wine, add ½ cup honey dissolved in 1 cup wine. Repeat process every six weeks until specific gravity is stable. Rack every month until wine is clear. Bottle when the wine is ready.

Even though dandelions can be a nuisance in a yard, they can make one of the best wines you will ever taste. Pick them when the yellow flowers are bloomed. You cannot use dandelions after they have gone to seed because they will be too bitter.

Dandy Lion Wine

Yield 1 Gallon/3.8 L

OG = 1.04 FG = 1.014 ABV = 10%

Ingredients:

- 1 gallon bucket full of dandelion flowers, fresh (You must watch carefully and pick just at the right time.)
- 5 ½ cups granulated sugar
- 1 tsp yeast nutrient
- 2 oranges, juice and rind
- 2 lemons, juice and rind
- 2 campden tablets
- 1 packet wine yeast
- Water
- Standard winemaking equipment
- 1-gallon carboy
- Nylon bag/cheesecloth

Instructions:

1. Pinch off any green calyces, which are the leaves around the bottom of the flower. Do not get any calyces or white sap in wine or it will make it very bitter. Place flowers in the bag/cloth and place bag in the primary fermenter. Add crushed campden tablets. Let sit for three days, stirring frequently.

2. Remove flower bag. Add lemon and orange juice with the grated rind. Dissolve in sugar and nutrients. Be sure the SG is between 1.100 and 1.110. Pitch yeast and stir. Stir four days until rapid fermentation ceases.

3. Strain and rack to carboy. Attach the airlock.

4. For a drier tasting wine, mature for at least three weeks, then rack and allow to mature four more weeks. The wine should be clear and the hydrometer readings stable before it is bottled.

5. For a sweeter tasting wine, mature for three weeks and then rack into another vessel. Dissolve ½ cup sugar in 1 cup of wine and pour the sweetened wine back into the fermentation vessel. Repeat this process until at least two hydrometer readings are stable, or every six weeks. Rack the wine every month until it is clear, then bottle.

6. For the best results, allow the wine to mature for at least two years from the date it was started before you drink it.

Dandier Lion Wine

Yield 1 Gallon/3.8 L

OG = 1.04 FG = 1.014 ABV = 10%

Ingredients:

- 4 cups dandelion flowers, fresh
- 1 lb raisins
- 1- to 4-inch cinnamon stick
- 5 ½ cups granulated sugar
- 1 tsp yeast nutrient
- 2 oranges, juice and rinds
- 2 lemons, juice and rinds
- 2 campden tablets
- 1 packet wine yeast
- Water
- Standard winemaking equipment
- 1-gallon carboy
- Nylon bag/cheesecloth

Instructions:

1. Pinch off any green calyces, which are the leaves around the bottom of the flower. Do not get any calyces or white sap in wine or it will make it very bitter. Place flowers in the bag/cloth. Add raisins and cinnamon stick to bag and place bag in the primary fermenter. Add crushed campden tablets. Let sit for three days, stirring frequently.

2. Remove flower bag. Add lemon and orange juice with the grated rind. Dissolve in sugar and nutrients. Be sure the SG is between 1.100 and 1.110. Pitch yeast and stir. Stir four days until rapid fermentation ceases.

3. Strain and rack to carboy. Attach the airlock.

4. For a drier tasting wine, mature for at least three weeks, then rack and allow to mature four more weeks. The wine should be clear and the hydrometer readings stable before it is bottled.

5. For a sweeter tasting wine, mature for three weeks and then rack into another vessel. Dissolve ½ cup sugar in 1 cup of wine and pour the sweetened wine back into the fermentation vessel. Repeat this process until at least two hydrometer readings are stable, or every six weeks. Rack the wine every month until it is clear, then bottle.

6. For the best results, allow the wine to mature for at least two years from the date it was started before you drink it.

Fireweed is an interesting plant. It gets its name from being one of the first flowers that will grow after a forest fire.

Light Me on Fire Wine

Yield 1 Gallon/3.8 L

OG = 1.100 FG = 1.014 ABV = 12%

Ingredients:

- 6 cups sugar
- ½ lb raisins
- 2 oranges, juice and rinds
- 8 cups fireweed blossoms
- 1 tsp nutrients
- 2 campden tablets
- 1 packet wine yeast
- Water
- Standard winemaking equipment
- 1-gallon carboy
- Nylon bag/cheesecloth

Instructions:

1. Bring ½ gallon water to a boil and dissolve in the sugar. Pour into fermentation bucket and add chopped raisins. Raise the level to 1 gallon with water and let sit 24 hours.

2. Make sure the SG is 1.100. Add fireweed flowers to bag. Add only the flowers; remove any stalks, leaves, or other green parts. Add all other ingredients including yeast. Stir daily for four days.

3. Remove bag and gently squeeze. Rack liquid into the carboy and attach an airlock.

4. For a drier tasting wine, mature for at least three weeks, then rack and allow to mature four more weeks. The wine should be clear and the hydrometer readings stable before it is bottled.

5. For a sweeter tasting wine, mature for three weeks and then rack into another vessel. Dissolve ½ cup sugar in 1 cup of wine and pour the sweetened wine back into the fermentation vessel. Repeat this process until at least two hydrometer readings are stable, or every six weeks. Rack the wine every month until it is clear, then bottle.

> "Patience, patience, patience! As long as the wine is not obviously spoiled, wait for it to clear and to improve in flavor."
> *Dave Schiedermayer, home winemaker*

This next wine contains herbs that may be a little more difficult to locate. You might be able to find them online or in an Asian market. If you cannot find all of the herbs, that is fine. The herbs are meant to give the wine a complex flavor and some believe the herbs have medicinal properties. Neither this wine nor any other wine in this book is meant to be used as a medicine. The information concerning their medicinal properties is only included for anecdotal purposes.

Lucky Dragon Wine

Yield 1 Gallon/3.8 L

OG = 1.122 FG = 0.090 ABV = 13%

Ingredients:

- 5 ½ cups granulated sugar
- 1 tsp yeast nutrient
- 2 oranges, juice and rinds
- 2 lemons, juice and rinds
- 8 oz peeled ginger, thin-sliced and soaked in honey
- 3 pods of cardamom seeds
- 2 limes thin-sliced
- 1 cup of raisins
- 1 tsp mace
- 1 stick of crushed cinnamon
- 1 tsp crushed cloves
- 1 nut of nutmeg, crushed
- 2 campden tablets
- 1 package champagne wine yeast
- Water
- Standard winemaking equipment
- 1-gallon carboy
- Nylon bag/cheesecloth

Herbal extract ingredients:

1 part each:

- Tang kuei
- Polygonum multiflorum
- Lychii fruit
- Schizandra berries
- Asparagi
- Rehmannia (processed)
- Licorice root
- Morindae
- Atractylodis

2 parts each:

- Chinese ginseng
- Astragalus
- American ginseng
- Jujube dates

½ part:

- Eucommia bark

Trace/Pinch:

- Peony root
- Gum frankincense
- Gum myrrh

Instructions

1. You will need to create the extract first. Place herbal extract ingredients into a cheesecloth. Simmer them in a quart of water for one hour. Pour off the water into fermenter. Repeat this until you have 3 quarts of water.

2. Boil a quart of water and dissolve the sugar. Add the fruit and other spices to cheesecloth and simmer for 30 minutes. Cool the must until it is room temperature and add to the fermenter.

3. Add the campden tablet and nutrient and stir well. Pitch the yeast. Allow to sit for 24 hours.

4. Pull out the cheesecloth. Allow to sit for two weeks. Strain and rack into a carboy and allow to sit for four weeks.

5. For a drier tasting wine, mature for at least three weeks, then rack and allow to mature four more weeks. The wine should be clear and the hydrometer readings stable before it is bottled.

6. For a sweeter tasting wine, mature for three weeks and then rack into another vessel. Dissolve ½ cup sugar in 1 cup of wine and pour the sweetened wine back into the fermentation vessel. Repeat this process until at least two hydrometer readings are stable, or every six weeks. Rack the wine every month until it is clear, then bottle.

Honeysuckle

Yield 1 Gallon/3.8 L

OG = 1.090 FG = 1.014 ABV = 10%

Ingredients:

- 4 cups honeysuckle blossoms (use only the flowers as the berries are poisonous)
- 5 ½ cups granulated sugar
- 2 oranges, juice and rind
- ½ lb raisins
- 2 tsp acid blend
- 1 tsp pectic enzyme
- Nylon bag/cheesecloth

- 1 campden tablet
- 1 tsp nutrients
- 1 tsp tannin
- Water
- 1 packet wine yeast
- Standard winemaking equipment
- 1-gallon carboy

Instructions:

1. Rinse the blossoms gently in cold water. Place in bag/cloth and then place bag in the primary fermenter. Raise the level of the must to 1 gallon by adding water and add remaining ingredients except yeast. Stir to dissolve sugar. Make sure the SG is between 1.090 and 1.100. Let sit 24 hours.

2. Add yeast and stir daily until rapid fermentation ceases.

3. Remove bag and gently squeeze out liquid. Rack liquid into the carboy and attach air lock.

4. For a drier tasting wine, mature for at least three weeks, then rack and allow maturing four more weeks. The wine should be clear and the hydrometer readings stable before it is bottled.

5. For a sweeter tasting wine, mature for three weeks and then rack into another vessel. Dissolve ½-cup sugar in 1 cup of wine and pour the sweetened wine back into the fermentation vessel. Repeat this process until at least two hydrometer readings are stable, or every six weeks. Rack the wine every month until it is clear, then bottle.

6. Mature wine for one year after the date the batch was started.

Be careful handling nettles as they can be very irritating to the skin. Use gloves when handling. When they are heated or dried, the irritation properties are removed.

Nettling Wine

Yield 1 Gallon/3.8 L

OG = 1.090 FG = 1.014 ABV = 10%

Ingredients:

- 8 cups nettle tops
- 1 lb raisins
- 6 ½ cups granulated sugar
- 1 tsp yeast nutrients
- 2 lemons or oranges (juice and rinds)
- 2 campden tablets
- Water
- 1 packet wine yeast
- Standard winemaking equipment
- 1-gallon carboy
- Nylon bag/cheesecloth

Instructions:

1. Look for the tender nettle tops in early spring. (Remember your gloves.) Rinse well and simmer the tops on low with citrus rind for 20 minutes. Place in bag and squeeze out all of the liquid into the

primary fermenter. Discard pulp. Raise the level of the must to 1 gallon by adding water. Add sugar, nutrients, raisins, citrus juice, and campden tablets. Stir the must in order to dissolve sugar. Let sit 24 hours.

2. Make sure the SG is between 1.090 and 1.100. Pitch yeast. Stir for three days or until rapid fermentation ceases. Rack into carboy and attach airlock.

3. For a drier tasting wine, mature for at least three weeks, then rack and allow maturing four more weeks. The wine should be clear and the hydrometer readings stable before it is bottled.

4. For a sweeter tasting wine, mature for three weeks and then rack into another vessel. Dissolve ½ cup sugar in 1 cup of wine and pour the sweetened wine back into the fermentation vessel. Repeat this process until at least two hydrometer readings are stable, or every six weeks. Rack the wine every month until it is clear, then bottle.

5. For the best results, allow the wine to mature for at least one year from the date it was started before you drink it.

Rosey Rose Wine

Yield 1 Gallon/3.8 L

OG = 1.090 FG = 1.014 ABV = 10%

Ingredients:

- 1 lb rose hips
- Water
- 6 cups sugar
- 1 ½ cups raisin
- Packet of yeast
- 1-gallon carboy
- Standard winemaking equipment

Instructions:

1. Grind up rose hips in a blender and place in cheesecloth/bag. Simmer the hips on low for 20 minutes. Squeeze out all of the liquid into the primary fermenter. Discard pulp. Raise the level of the must to 1 gallon by adding water. Add sugar and raisins. Stir the must in order to dissolve sugar. Let sit 24 hours.

2. Make sure the SG is between 1.090 and 1.100. Pitch yeast. Stir for three days or until rapid fermentation ceases. Rack into carboy and attach airlock.

3. For a drier tasting wine, mature for at least three weeks, then rack and allow maturing four more weeks. The wine should be clear and the hydrometer readings stable before it is bottled.

4. For a sweeter tasting wine, mature for three weeks and then rack into another vessel. Dissolve ½ cup sugar in 1 cup of wine and pour the sweetened wine back into the fermentation vessel. Repeat this process until at least two hydrometer readings are stable, or every six weeks. Rack the wine every month until it is clear, then bottle.

5. For the best results, allow the wine to mature for at least one year from the date it was started before you drink it.

Cat's Tale Wine

Yield 1 Gallon/3.8 L
OG = 1.090 FG = 1.014 ABV = 10%

Ingredients:

- 5 lbs of cattail spikes (upper male flower spike)
- 1 orange
- 1 lemon

- Water
- 8 cups sugar
- 1 ½ cups raisin
- 1 ½ cups course ground corn meal
- 1 packet wine yeast
- 1-gallon carboy
- Nylon bag/cheesecloth
- Standard winemaking equipment

Instructions:

1. Clean dirt from cattails. Scrub it well and slice it. Place cattails in cheesecloth/bag. Squeeze juice from lemon and orange into fermenter. Place the peel and rind in the cheesecloth. Simmer the cattails on low for 20 minutes in 3 quarts of water. Squeeze out all of the liquid into the primary fermenter. Discard pulp. Raise the level of the must to 1 gallon by adding water. Add sugar, raisins, and cornmeal. Stir the must in order to dissolve sugar. Let sit 24 hours.

2. Make sure the SG is between 1.090 and 1.100. Pitch yeast. Stir for three days or until rapid fermentation ceases. Rack into carboy and attach airlock.

3. For a drier tasting wine, mature for at least three weeks, then rack and allow maturing four more weeks. The wine should be clear and the hydrometer readings stable before it is bottled.

4. For a sweeter tasting wine, mature for three weeks and then rack into another vessel. Dissolve ½ cup sugar in 1 cup of wine and pour the sweetened wine back into the fermentation vessel. Repeat this process until at least two hydrometer readings are stable, or every six weeks. Rack the wine every month until it is clear, then bottle.

5. For the best results, allow the wine to mature for at least one year from the date it was started before you drink it.

CHAPTER 7

Meads

Meads are one of the most ancient brews on earth. Legend has it that honey once dripped from a honeycomb into water, and natural yeasts fermented the draught. Then, according to legend, some brave individual drank it.

Mead is essentially honey wine. It uses honey as its sugar source, although the type of honey imparts certain flavors, aromas, and colors to the wine. Each type of honey is produced by bees that have different flower sources. For instance, bees in certain parts of Florida and California live or are placed near orange groves. The nectar and other flower parts are brought back to the hive by the bee. The orange nectar and flower then become part of the honey. It gives a light orange flavor and color and therefore is referred to as orange blossom honey.

You can experiment with all different types of honey. You can mix and match. Natural Health practitioners often state that if you eat local honey that you will cure many of your hay fever difficulties. Like wine and cider, there are different forms of mead: sweet, dry, still, and sparkling. Mead is also broken up into other specific categories according to what types of ingredients are added to it. Even though mead can stand on its own as a delicious drink, there are many other combinations of ingredients that make this type of wild wine special.

This chart names the types of mead and the types of ingredients.

NAME OF MEAD	INGREDIENTS
Simple Mead	Contains honey. There many be other ingredients such as citrus fruit, but these are added to raise the acid level, rather than to be a major component of flavor.
Sack Mead	Contains extra honey, although may contain other ingredients as well.
Melomels	Fruit
Metheglins	Herbs and Spices
Rhodamels	Flowers
Rhizamels	Vegetables
Pyment	Grape Juice
Braggot	Hops
Black Mead	Black Currants
Capsicumel	Chile Peppers
Cyser	Apple Juice
Morat	Mulberries

Simple Mead

Yield 5 gallons/19 L
OG=1.14 FG=1.045 ABV=10%

Ingredients:

- 18 lbs wildflower honey
- 2 cups New York maple syrup - Grade A
- 32 oz fresh lemon and lime juice (some pulp)
- 12 lemons
- 8 limes
- 4 pieces (⅛ fruit) orange peel
- 5 pieces tangerine peel
- 3 pieces lemon peel
- 2 oz coriander
- Water
- Sweet mead yeast
- ½ tsp gypsum
- ½ tsp calcium carbonate
- ¼ tsp sea salt
- Standard winemaking equipment

Instructions:

1. Boil about 4 gallons of water. Treat it with gypsum, calcium carbonate, and sea salt. Boil it for 30 minutes. Take off the heat and add orange peels, lime peels, and ½ oz coriander. Allow the mixture to cool to 194 degrees F/90 degrees C. Add honey and maple syrup. Allow temperature to drop to 176 degrees F/80 degrees C. Add strained juice from six lemons and four limes.

2. Stir for 30 minutes. Raise temperature back up to 194 degrees F/90 degrees C. Add juice with pulp then add six more lemons and four limes.

3. Reduce the temperature of mixture either by ice bath or wort chiller. Reduce temperature quickly and place in primary fermenter. Raise level of water to 5 gallons and allow to ferment for two weeks.

4. Rack to carboy. Allow to sit for two months. Bottle.

5. The longer you allow it to mature the smoother the taste.

Melomels

These meads are made with different kinds of fruits. The honey provides some of the flavor, although there is much sweetness and flavor that comes from the fruits as well.

Cranky Berry Melomel

Yield 1 Gallon/3.8 L

OG = 1.090 FG = 1.014 ABV = 10%

Ingredients:

- 2 lbs local orange blossom honey
- 1 lb local sage honey
- 24 oz cranberries
- Pectic enzyme
- Water
- Sweet mead yeast
- 1-gallon carboy
- Standard winemaking equipment
- Cheesecloth/nylon bag

Instructions:

1. If you are using frozen cranberries make sure that they are thawed. Place honey in a pot with 3 quarts of water and boil for 20 minutes. Skim foam off the top.

2. Place cranberries in cheesecloth in the fermenter and pour honey mixture over the top. Try to cool the mixture quickly. Add pectic enzyme.

3. When the must reaches room temperature pitch, the yeast. Allow it to ferment for three weeks.

4. Rack the mead off the bag and squeeze juice gently from the cheesecloth.

5. For dry mead, allow the mead to sit in a dark, cool place for four to six months. Rack every three weeks until mead is clear. Bottle when wine is ready.

6. If you wish to add carbonation, you can add ¼ tsp white table sugar per 12 oz bottle, or stir in ½ lb to 1 lb raw honey. You will want to dissolve the honey in boiling water first and cool it. Rack every three weeks until mead is clear.

7. Allow mead to age for six months to a year.

Rub a Dub Melomel

Yield 1 Gallon/3.8 L

OG = 1.092 FG = 1.014 ABV = 10%

Ingredients:

- 3 lbs wildflower honey
- Water
- 1 tsp yeast nutrient
- 7 cups chopped fresh rhubarb (you can also use frozen)
- 1-gallon carboy
- Cheesecloth/nylon bag
- Sweet mead yeast
- Standard winemaking equipment

Instructions:

1. If you are using frozen rhubarb, make sure that they are thawed. Place honey in a pot with 3 quarts of water and boil for 20 minutes. Skim foam off the top.

2. Place rhubarb in cheesecloth in the fermenter and pour honey mixture over the top. Try to cool the mixture quickly. Add pectic enzyme.

3. When the must reaches room temperature pitch the yeast. Allow it to ferment for three weeks.

4. Rack the mead off the bag and squeeze juice gently from the cheesecloth.

5. For dry mead, allow the mead to sit in a dark, cool place for four to six months. Rack every three weeks until mead is clear. Bottle when wine is ready.

6. If you wish to add carbonation, you can add ¼ tsp of white table sugar per 12 oz bottle, or stir in ½ lb to 1 lb raw of honey. You will want to dissolve the honey in boiling water first and cool it. Rack every three weeks until mead is clear.

7. Allow mead to age for six months to a year.

Raspy Melomel

Yield 1 Gallon/3.8 L

OG = 1.092 FG = 1.014 ABV = 10%

Ingredients:

- 12 lbs light clover honey
- 2 gallons black raspberries
- 1 oz dried raspberry leaves
- 4 tsp citric acid
- 1 package champagne yeast
- 1 lb white sugar
- 1 campden tablet
- 1-gallon carboy
- Standard winemaking equipment
- Water
- Cheesecloth/nylon bag

Instructions:

1. Boil honey in a pot with 3 quarts of water. Bring honey, raspberry leaves, citric acid, and 1 gallon water to a full boil. Skim off any foam that forms.

2. Place berries in the cheesecloth/bag. If you used frozen berries make sure that they are thawed before using. Pour honey mixture over the berries, add campden tablet, and allow it to sit 24 hours.

3. Pitch yeast and allow to ferment for at least three weeks or when primary fermentation has ceased. Take out the berries and gently squeeze the bag of any remaining juice.

4. Rack wine into carboy and attach fermentation lock.

5. For dry mead, allow the mead to sit in a dark, cool place for four to six months. Rack every three weeks until mead is clear. Bottle when wine is ready.

6. If you wish to add carbonation, you can add ¼ tsp of white table sugar per 12 oz bottle, or stir in ½ lb to 1 lb raw of honey. You will want to dissolve the honey in boiling water first and cool it. Rack every three weeks until mead is clear.

7. Allow mead to age for six months to a year.

Screaming John's Halloween Mead

This is one of my favorite mead recipes. It not only tastes great, but it is a lot of fun to make. This is great to make for a Halloween party. You may consider making this toward the end of summer or for Halloween the next year. Follow the directions carefully, because the directions for creating this mead are quite different from other recipes in this book.

Yield 1 Gallon/3.8 L

OG = 1.092 FG = 1.014 ABV = 10%

Ingredients:

- 1 firm, medium-sized pumpkin
- Paraffin wax
- Water
- 4 lbs light honey
- 2 oranges
- 2 lemons
- Dry mead yeast
- 1 tea bag (black tea)
- 1-gallon carboy
- Cheesecloth/nylon bag
- Old bucket or fermenter large enough to dip pumpkin
- A large paraffin candle
- Rubber gloves

Instructions:

1. Boil ½ gallon water and add honey. Continue to boil for 20 minutes. Skim off any foam that forms.

2. Remove mixture from the heat. Cut the fruit into pieces and add to cheesecloth. Place bag into honey mixture. Allow the mixture to cool to room temperature. Pitch yeast. Place in a covered container (fermenter) overnight.

3. Cut a hole in the top of the pumpkin like you would when making a jack-o-lantern. Make sure the piece you cut fits snuggly back on top. Use a spoon or ice cream scoop to scrape out the seeds and strings inside the pumpkin. Do not cut any other holes in the pumpkin.

4. Boil some water and use it to rinse out the pumpkin.

5. Pour the must that you created the night before into the pumpkin. Remove the bag and squeeze the juice into the pumpkin. You must leave an inch of air space between the liquid and the top of the pumpkin. Fit the top back on top of the pumpkin.

6. Find a large bucket or an old plastic fermenter large enough to dip your pumpkin into.

7. Prepare the area you are working in. It is better to do the pumpkin dipping outside in case the wax drips. You may want to line the area you are working in with newspaper.

8. Boil the water. Place paraffin in the bucket and pour hot water over it to melt it. The wax will float to the top of the water.

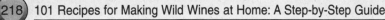

9. While the water is still hot, dip the pumpkin into the paraffin. Put on gloves to protect your hands. Start at the bottom first and make sure it is coated all the way to the rim, bottom first, into the warm paraffin until it is coated up to its lid. Make sure the entire pumpkin up to the rim is sealed in paraffin.

10. Light the candle and drip wax on the seam to seal the pumpkin lid. Once you are sure it is sealed, turn the pumpkin over and dip in the bucket to seal the top of the pumpkin in wax. You must do this process quickly as the paraffin will begin to cool and harden in the bucket. If this happens, pour out the water and boil more water to melt the wax again. Make sure you are wearing gloves at all times to prevent burning your hands.

11. Place the pumpkin in a shallow pan of water. This prevents worms from invading your pumpkin. Place in cool, dark place to ferment. Some people who have tried this recipe have used a net to hang the pumpkin up instead of using a pan. Allow to ferment for two months.

12. Rack into a carboy by poking a hole in the top of the pumpkin. Be careful because the pumpkin may be soft. Allow to sit for a few more weeks before bottling to ensure fermentation has ceased. You may even consider adding some campden tablets before bottling.

13. The longer you allow it to age, the better it will be.

No Fruit Allowed Raspberry Mead

I made this mead and it was gone quickly. I created it in memorial of a friend's cat passing and placed a picture of the cat on the label. The best part is that it had a strong raspberry flavor without the need to buy expensive raspberries.

Yield 1 Gallon/3.8 L

OG = 1.092 FG = 1.014 ABV = 10%

Ingredients:

- 4 ½ lbs wildflower honey
- Bottle of raspberry extract
- Juice of one lemon
- Juice of one orange
- 3 tbsp of strong-brewed black English tea
- 1 campden tablet
- 1 tsp yeast nutrient (generic, white crystals)
- Water
- Sweet mead
- Standard winemaking equipment
- 1-gallon carboy

Instructions:

1. Boil the honey in 3 quarts of water. Skim off foam as it forms. Remove from heat and add tea, juice, and nutrients. Allow to cool for 24 hours.

2. Pitch the yeast and transfer to carboy.

3. Allow to ferment for three weeks and rack off the sediment.

4. If you wish to add carbonation, you can add ¼ tsp of white table sugar per 12 oz bottle, or stir in ½ lb to 1 lb raw of honey. You will want to dissolve the honey in boiling water first and cool it. Rack every three weeks until mead is clear.

5. Once you are sure the mead is stable, add a campden tablet and raspberry extract. Allow to sit for another week. Take hydrometer readings to make sure the mead has not refermented. Bottle.

6. Allow this mead to mature three to six months before drinking.

The first time I created this mead I did not add the campden tablet or make sure that it was stable. The result was fountains of pink liquid.

Seedy Cyser

Yield 1 Gallon/3.8 L

OG = 1.092 FG = 1.014 ABV = 10%

Ingredients:

- 1 gallon strained kiwi puree
- 2 gallons apple juice
- Water
- 3 cups cane sugar
- 6 lbs clover honey
- 6 tsp acid blend
- 1 ½ tsp yeast nutrient
- 3 campden tablets
- Standard winemaking equipment
- Champagne yeast

Instructions:

1. Boil the honey in 3 quarts of water. Skim off foam as it forms. Remove from heat and add all of the ingredients except the yeast. Allow to cool for 24 hours.

2. Pitch the yeast and transfer to carboy.

3. Allow to ferment for three weeks and rack off the sediment.

4. For dry mead, allow the mead to sit in a dark, cool place for four to six months. Rack every three weeks until mead is clear. Bottle when wine is ready.

5. If you wish to add carbonation, you can add ¼ tsp of white table sugar per 12 oz bottle, or stir in ½ lb to 1 lb raw of honey. You

will want to dissolve the honey in boiling water first and cool it. Rack every three weeks until mead is clear.

6. Allow mead to age for six months to a year.

Palm of Granite Melomel

Yield: 5 gallons/19 L

OG = 1.100 FG = 1.010 ABV = 12%

Ingredients:

- 10 lbs orange blossom honey
- 5 lbs wildflower honey
- 2 tsp yeast nutrient
- Champagne yeast
- Water
- Standard winemaking equipment
- 1 gallon of pomegranate juice (can be pure juice from the store or made from 14 lbs of pomegranates)
- 1 campden tablet

Instructions:

1. Boil the honey in 3 quarts of water. Skim off foam as it forms. Remove from heat and add all the ingredients except the yeast and pomegranate juice. Allow to cool for 24 hours.

2. Pitch the yeast and transfer to carboy.

3. Allow to ferment for three weeks and rack off the sediment.

4. Boil pomegranate juice for ten minutes. If you are using fresh pomegranates you must squeeze the juice and discard the seeds and

pitch. This can be a little labor intensive. Add a campden tablet and juice to the mead. Bring level of water up to 5 gallons.

5. For dry mead, allow the mead to sit in a dark, cool place for four to six months. Rack every three weeks until mead is clear. Bottle when wine is ready.

6. If you wish to add carbonation, you can add ¼ tsp of white table sugar per 12 oz bottle, or stir in ½ lb to 1 lb raw of honey. You will want to dissolve the honey in boiling water first and cool it. Rack every three weeks until mead is clear.

7. Allow mead to age for six months to a year.

Strawberry Shortcake Melomel

Yield 1 Gallon/3.8 L

OG = 1.092 FG = 1.014 ABV = 10%

Ingredients:

- 10 lbs citrus honey
- 2 tsp yeast energizer
- 10 lbs frozen strawberries
- 2 sticks of cinnamon
- ½ tsp ground mace
- Champagne yeast
- Standard winemaking equipment
- Water

Instructions:

1. Boil the honey in 2 quarts of water. Skim off foam as it forms. Add yeast energizer. Allow to cool for 24 hours.

2. Pitch the yeast and transfer to carboy.

3. Allow to ferment for three weeks and rack off the sediment.

4. Boil strawberries and spices in a quart of water. Add the mixture to the mead.

5. For dry mead, allow the mead to sit in a dark, cool place for four to six months. Rack every three weeks until mead is clear. Bottle when wine is ready.

6. If you wish to add carbonation, you can add ¼ tsp white table sugar per 12 oz bottle, or stir in ½ lb to 1 lb raw honey. Dissolve the honey in boiling water first and cool. Rack every three weeks until mead is clear.

7. Allow mead to age for six months to a year.

Spicy Sun Melomel

Yield: 5 gallons/19 L

OG = 1.100 FG = 1.010 ABV = 12%

Ingredients:

- 20 lbs dark honey
- 2 lbs raisins
- 2 tbsp whole cloves (do not use ground clove)
- 1 oz citric acid
- 1 packet wine yeast
- 1 campden tablet
- Water
- Cheesecloth/nylon bag
- Standard winemaking equipment

Instructions:

1. Boil honey in a pot with 3 quarts of water. Bring honey, citric acid, and 1 gallon water to a full boil. Skim off any foam that forms.

2. Place raisins and cloves in the cheesecloth/bag. Pour honey mixture over the bag; add campden tablet and citric acid. Allow it to sit 24 hours.

3. Bring water level up to 5 gallons. Pitch yeast and allow to ferment for at least three weeks or when primary fermentation has ceased. Take out the bag and gently squeeze the bag of any remaining juice.

4. Rack wine into carboy and attach fermentation lock.

5. For dry mead, allow the mead to sit in a dark, cool place for four to six months. Rack every three weeks until mead is clear. Bottle when wine is ready.

6. If you wish to add carbonation, you can add ¼ tsp white table sugar per 12 oz bottle, or stir in ½ lb to 1 lb raw honey. Dissolve the honey in boiling water first and cool. Rack every three weeks until mead is clear.

7. Allow mead to age for six months to a year.

Orange You Glad It's a Melomel

Yield 1 Gallon/3.8 L

OG = 1.092 FG = 1.014 ABV = 10%

Ingredients:

- 5 lbs clover honey
- 1 lb Tupelo honey
- Juice from one orange
- Orange zest with pith removed from one orange
- ⅓ tsp nutmeg
- 1 tsp gypsum
- 1 tsp yeast nutrient
- 1 tsp yeast energizer
- 1 packet Red Star Flor Sherry yeast
- Standard winemaking equipment
- Water
- 1-gallon carboy

Instructions:

1. Boil honey in a pot with 3 quarts of water for 20 minutes. Skim off any foam that forms. Remove from heat. Add gypsum, zest, nutmeg, and nutrient and energizer to the must. Allow it to sit 24 hours.

2. Pitch yeast and allow to ferment for at least three weeks or when primary fermentation has ceased. Add juice to the must.

3. Rack wine into carboy and attach fermentation lock.

4. For dry mead, allow the mead to sit in a dark, cool place for four to six months. Rack every three weeks until mead is clear. Bottle when wine is ready.

5. If you wish to add carbonation, you can add ¼ tsp white table sugar per 12 oz bottle, or stir in ½ lb to 1 lb raw honey. Dissolve the honey in boiling water first and cool. Rack every three weeks until mead is clear.

6. Allow mead to age for six months to a year.

Plum Good Melomel

Yield 5 Gallon/19 L

OG = 1.092 FG = 1.014 ABV = 10%

Ingredients:

- 10 lbs wildflower honey
- 12 lbs fresh plums pitted with skins on
- 3 oz acid blend
- 1 packet American Ale yeast
- Water
- 1-gallon carboy
- Cheesecloth/nylon bag
- Standard winemaking equipment

Instructions:

1. Boil honey in a pot with 3 quarts of water for 20 minutes. Skim off any foam that forms. Remove from heat. Add the plums to cheesecloth/ bag and place in fermenter with honey mixture. Allow it to sit 24 hours.

2. Pitch yeast and allow to ferment for at least three weeks or when primary fermentation has ceased. Remove bag and gently squeeze out the juice.

3. Rack wine into carboy and attach fermentation lock.

4. For dry mead, allow the mead to sit in a dark, cool place for four to six months. Rack every three weeks until mead is clear. Bottle when wine is ready.

5. If you wish to add carbonation, you can add ¼ tsp white table sugar per 12 oz bottle, or stir in ½ lb to 1 lb raw honey. Dissolve the honey in boiling water first and cool. Rack every three weeks until mead is clear.

6. Allow mead to age for six months to a year.

April Bed Melomel

Yield 1 Gallon/3.8 L

OG = 1.127 FG = 1.023 ABV = 13.95%

Ingredients:

- 5.47 lb Questa honey
- 0.55 lb Sourwood honey
- 0.10 lb Star Thistle honey
- 1.47 lb Clover honey
- 9.0 lb apricot juice
- 2 packages Lalvin K1V-1116 (Montpelier) wine yeast
- 2 campden tablets
- ½ tsp. acid blend
- Water
- 1-gallon carboy
- Standard winemaking equipment

Instructions:

1. Remove the pits from the apricots and puree. Freeze the pulp for about a week. Allow it to thaw before you use it in the mead. Squeeze juice using a press or cheesecloth.

2. Boil Questa, Sourwood, and Star Thistle honey and apricot juice in ½ gallon of water for 20 minutes. Skim off the foam that forms. Stir in acid blend. Allow to cool overnight.

3. Pitch yeast and allow to ferment for at least three weeks or when primary fermentation has ceased.

4. Rack wine into carboy and attach fermentation lock.

5. For dry mead, allow the mead to sit in a dark, cool place for four to six months. Rack every three weeks until mead is clear. Bottle when wine is ready.

6. If you wish to add carbonation, you can add ¼ tsp white table sugar per 12 oz bottle, or stir in ½ lb to 1 lb raw honey. Dissolve the honey in boiling water first and cool. Rack every three weeks until mead is clear.

7. Allow mead to age for six months to a year.

Dazzling Strawberry Mead

Yield: 5 gallons/19 L

OG = 1.100 FG =1.010 ABV = 12%

Ingredients:

- 15 lbs sage honey
- 8 lbs fresh strawberries (destemmed, washed, and pureed)
- 2 tsp Irish moss
- 6 tbsp vanilla extract • Water
- 1 packet Ale yeast* • Standard winemaking
- Yeast nutrient   equipment

Instructions:

1. Remove the stems and leaves from strawberries and puree in a food processor. Freeze the pulp for about a week. Allow it to thaw before you use it in the mead. Put puree in a cheesecloth and place in fermenter.

2. Boil honey in a half gallon of water 20 minutes. Skim off the foam the forms. Stir in Irish moss. Allow to cool overnight.

3. Bring water level up to 5 gallons. Pitch yeast and nutrients. Allow to ferment for at least three weeks or when primary fermentation has ceased.

4. Rack wine into carboy and attach fermentation lock.

5. For dry mead, allow the mead to sit in a dark, cool place for four to six months. Rack every three weeks until mead is clear. Bottle when wine is ready.

6. If you wish to add carbonation, you can add ¼ tsp white table sugar per 12 oz bottle, or stir in ½ lb to 1 lb raw honey. Dissolve the honey in boiling water first and cool. Rack every three weeks until mead is clear.

7. Allow mead to age for six months to a year.

You can find ale yeast wherever winemaking and beer making supplies are sold. This gives this mead a slightly different character and may do better as drier mead.

Funky Banana Mead

Yield 1 Gallon/ 3.8 L

OG = 1.127 FG = 1.023 ABV = 13.95%

Ingredients:

- 3 lb ripe bananas
- 8 oz Johannesburg Riesling Grape concentrate
- 1 oz whole ginger
- 5 oz clove
- Water
- 2 ½ lbs honey
- 2 ½ tsp acid blend
- 5 tsp tannin
- 5 tsp yeast energizer
- 1 packet of Red Star Cote De Blanc yeast
- Cheesecloth/nylon bag
- 1-gallon carboy
- Standard winemaking equipment

Instructions:

1. Cut up the bananas with the skins intact and place them in cheese-cloth/bag. Place them in pot and boil them for 30 minutes. Discard pulp.

2. Pour honey and hot banana water into a fermenter. Mix until the honey dissolves. Place ginger and whole clove in a cheesecloth/bag and add to fermenter. Add acid blend, tannin, grape juice, and energizer to the mixture and stir well. Allow the mixture to cool overnight.

3. Pitch yeast and allow to ferment for at least three weeks or when primary fermentation has ceased.

4. Rack wine into carboy and attach fermentation lock.

5. For dry mead, allow the mead to sit in a dark, cool place for four to six months. Rack every three weeks until mead is clear. Bottle when wine is ready.

6. If you wish to add carbonation, you can add ¼ tsp white table sugar per 12 oz bottle, or stir in ½ lb to 1 lb raw honey. Dissolve the honey in boiling water first and cool. Rack every three weeks until mead is clear.

7. Allow mead to age for six months to a year.

Rhubarb Melomel

Yield 5 Gallon/19 L

OG = 1.080 FG = 0.0994 ABV = 14%

Ingredients:

- 11 lbs honey
- 8 to10 lbs rhubarb chopped (no leaves)
- 2 ½ tsp nutrient
- ¼ tsp tannin
- Champagne yeast
- Water
- Cheesecloth/ nylon bag
- 1-gallon carboy
- Standard winemaking equipment

Instructions:

1. Cut up rhubarb. Discard any leaves as these can be poisonous. Freeze the fruit for about a week. Allow it to thaw before you use it in the mead. Put cut up rhubarb in a cheesecloth and place in fermenter.

2. Boil honey in ½ gallon of water for 20 minutes. Skim off the foam the forms. Stir in nutrient and tannin. Allow to cool overnight.

3. Pitch yeast and allow to ferment for at least three weeks or when primary fermentation has ceased. Remove rhubarb bag and gently squeeze juice.

4. Rack wine into carboy and attach fermentation lock.

5. For dry mead, allow the mead to sit in a dark, cool place for four to six months. Rack every three weeks until mead is clear. Bottle when wine is ready.

6. If you wish to add carbonation, you can add ¼ tsp white table sugar per 12 oz bottle, or stir in ½ lb to 1 lb raw honey. Dissolve the honey in boiling water first and cool. Rack every three weeks until mead is clear.

7. Allow mead to age for six months to a year.

Sour Drop Sima

A Sima is a simple mead created in Finland. It is often seasoned with lemon and is closely associated with the festival of Vappu, also known as Walpurgis Night or May Day. It is celebrated on May 1.

Yield 1 Gallon/3.8 L

OG = 1.080 FG = 0.0994 ABV = 14%

Ingredients:

- 43 oz lemon juice
- 2 lbs mixed honey
- Yeast nutrient
- ½ oz tartaric acid
- Water
- Cheesecloth/nylon bag
- 1-gallon carboy
- Standard winemaking equipment
- Bordeaux yeast

Instructions:

1. Boil honey in ½ gallon of water for 20 minutes. Skim off the foam the forms. Stir in lemon juice, nutrient, and tartaric acid. Allow to cool overnight.

2. Pitch yeast and allow to ferment for at least three weeks or when primary fermentation has ceased.

3. Rack wine into carboy and attach fermentation lock.

4. For dry mead, allow the mead to sit in a dark, cool place for four to six months. Rack every three weeks until mead is clear. Bottle when wine is ready.

5. If you wish to add carbonation, you can add ¼ tsp white table sugar per 12 oz bottle, or stir in ½ lb to 1 lb raw honey. Dissolve the honey in boiling water first and cool. Rack every three weeks until mead is clear.

6. Allow mead to age for six months to a year.

Fuzzy Was He?

Yield: 5 gallons/19 L

OG = 1.100 FG = 1.010 ABV = 12%

Ingredients:

- 15 lb Star Thistle honey
- 1 ½ oz yeast nutrient
- Water
- 35 lbs peaches

- Sweet mead yeast
- 1 tbsp pectic enzyme
- Cheesecloth/nylon bag
- Standard winemaking equipment

Instructions:

1. Remove the peach pits and boil peaches for five minutes in a gallon of water. Remove the skins and place pulp in a cheesecloth. Place cloth in fermenter. Do not discard peach water.

2. Bring peach water to a boil and stir in and dissolve honey. Skim off any foam that forms. Boil honey in ½ gallon of water for 20 minutes. Stir in nutrient and enzyme. Pour over peach bag in fermenter. Allow to cool overnight.

3. Bring liquid level up to 5 gallons. Pitch yeast and allow to ferment for at least three weeks or when primary fermentation has ceased. Remove peach bag and gently squeeze juice.

4. Rack wine into carboy and attach fermentation lock.

5. For dry mead, allow the mead to sit in a dark, cool place for four to six months. Rack every three weeks until mead is clear. Bottle when wine is ready.

6. If you wish to add carbonation, you can add ¼ tsp white table sugar per 12 oz bottle, or stir in ½ lb to 1 lb raw honey. Dissolve the honey in boiling water first and cool. Rack every three weeks until mead is clear.

7. Allow mead to age for six months to a year.

Goddess Ambrosia Mead

Yield: 5 gallons/19 L

OG = 1.100 FG = 1.010 ABV = 12%

Ingredients:

- 14 ½ lbs orange blossom honey
- Water
- 2 pineapples, peeled and chunked
- 4 mangoes, peeled and chunked
- 1 tangerine, sliced and seeded
- 2 cups dried cranberries (Make sure they do not contain sulfites. Look for organic)
- 7 oz ginger juice
- 1 cup of strong black tea
- Zest of 2 limes
- Zest of 3 oranges
- Yeast energizer tablets
- 2 packets Premier Couvee yeast
- Nylon bag/cheesecloth
- Standard winemaking equipment

Instructions:

1. Peel and remove pits from the fruit. Place pineapple, mangoes, tangerines, and cranberries in a cheesecloth/bag. Place bag in a pot and boil in 1 gallon of water for 10 minutes. Place bag in the fermenter, but keep the water in the pot.

2. Bring fruit water to a boil and stir in and dissolve honey. Skim off any foam that forms. Boil honey in ½ gallon of water for 20 minutes. Remove from heat. Boil a cup of tea and add tea to the mixture. Add zest, energizer, and juice to mixture then pour liquid over the fruit bag in the fermenter. Add water to bring the volume up to 5 gallons. Allow to cool overnight.

3. Pitch yeast and allow to ferment for at least three weeks or when primary fermentation has ceased. Remove fruit bag and gently squeeze juice.

4. Rack wine into carboy and attach fermentation lock.

5. For dry mead, allow the mead to sit in a dark, cool place for four to six months. Rack every three weeks until mead is clear. Bottle when wine is ready.

6. If you wish to add carbonation, you can add ¼ tsp white table sugar per 12 oz bottle, or stir in ½-lb to 1 lb raw honey. Dissolve the honey in boiling water first and cool. Rack every three weeks until mead is clear.

7. Allow mead to age for six months to a year.

Light Me Up Mead

Yield 5 Gallon/19 L

OG = 1.082 FG = 1.020 ABV = 10%

Ingredients:

- 11 ½ lbs wildflower honey
- 6 oz macerated ginger
- 12 oz can frozen orange juice
- Water
- Lalvin EC-1118 yeast
- 1-gallon carboy
- Standard winemaking equipment

Instructions:

1. Bring 3 quarts of water to a boil and stir in and dissolve honey. Skim off any foam that forms. Boil honey in ½ gallon of water for twenty minutes. Remove from heat. Add ginger and juice to mixture, and

then pour liquid over the fruit bag in the fermenter. Add water to bring the volume up to 5 gallons. Allow to cool overnight.

2. Pitch yeast and allow to ferment for at least three weeks or when primary fermentation has ceased.

3. Rack wine into carboy and attach fermentation lock.

4. For dry mead, allow the mead to sit in a dark, cool place for four to six months. Rack every three weeks until mead is clear. Bottle when wine is ready.

5. If you wish to add carbonation, you can add ¼ tsp white table sugar per 12 oz bottle, or stir in ½ lb to 1 lb raw honey. Dissolve the honey in boiling water first and cool. Rack every three weeks until mead is clear.

6. Allow mead to age for six months to a year.

Cherry-O Mead

Yield: 5 gallons/19 L

OG = 1.090 FG = 1.010 ABV = 10%

Ingredients:

- 5 ½ gallons unsweetened sour cherry juice
- 7 lbs crushed blueberries
- 2 ½ tsp yeast nutrient
- 2 ½ tsp yeast energizer
- 5 lbs clover honey
- 5 lbs wildflower honey
- Standard winemaking equipment

Instructions:

1. Crush blueberries and place in cheesecloth/bag. Place bag in a pot and boil in 1 gallon water for 10 minutes. Place bag in the fermenter, but keep the water in the pot.

2. Bring fruit water to a boil and stir in and dissolve honey. Skim off any foam that forms. Boil honey in ½ gallon water for 20 minutes. Remove from heat. Add nutrient, energizer, and juice to mixture, and then pour liquid over the fruit bag in the fermenter. Add water to bring the volume up to 5 gallons. Allow to cool overnight.

3. Pitch yeast and allow to ferment for at least three weeks or when primary fermentation has ceased. Remove fruit bag and gently squeeze juice.

4. Rack wine into carboy and attach fermentation lock.

5. For dry mead, allow the mead to sit in a dark, cool place for four to six months. Rack every three weeks until mead is clear. Bottle when wine is ready.

6. If you wish to add carbonation, you can add ¼ tsp white table sugar per 12 oz bottle, or stir in ½ lb to 1 lb raw honey. Dissolve the honey in boiling water first and cool. Rack every three weeks until mead is clear.

7. Allow mead to age for six months to a year.

Sunshine State Mead

Yield 1 Gallon/3.8 L

OG = 1.082 FG = 1.020 ABV = 10%

Ingredients:

- 4 lbs orange blossom honey
- Water
- 1 packet champagne yeast
- Citrus peels
- 2 cups freshly squeezed orange or tangerine juice
- Standard winemaking equipment

Instructions:

1. Bring 3 quarts of water to a boil and stir in and dissolve honey. Skim off any foam that forms. Boil honey in ½ gallon water for 20 minutes. Remove from heat. Add peels and juice to mixture then pour liquid over the fruit bag in the fermenter. Add water to bring the volume up to 5 gallons. Allow to cool overnight.

2. Pitch yeast and allow to ferment for at least three weeks or when primary fermentation has ceased.

3. Rack wine into carboy and attach fermentation lock.

4. For dry mead, allow the mead to sit in a dark, cool place for four to six months. Rack every three weeks until mead is clear. Bottle when wine is ready.

5. If you wish to add carbonation, you can add ¼ tsp white table sugar per 12 oz bottle, or stir in ½ lb to 1 lb raw honey. Dissolve the honey in boiling water first and cool. Rack every three weeks until mead is clear.

6. Allow mead to age for six months to a year.

Mango Cha Cha Mead

Yield 1 Gallon/3.8 L

OG = 1.082 FG =1.020 ABV = 10%

Ingredients:

- 3 lbs wildflower honey
- 2 large mangoes, frozen, then skinned and chunked
- ½ tsp pectic enzyme
- ½ tsp acid blend
- 1 tsp yeast nutrient
- Water
- Mead yeast packet
- Standard winemaking equipment
- 1-gallon carboy

Instructions:

1. Cut and skin frozen mangoes. Place the chunks in a cheesecloth/ bag. Place bag in a pot and boil in a gallon of water for 10 minutes. Place bag in the fermenter, but keep the water in the pot.

2. Bring fruit water to a boil and stir in and dissolve honey. Skim off any foam that forms. Boil honey in ½ gallon of water for 20 minutes. Remove from heat. Add nutrient, acid blend, pectic enzyme, and juice to mixture, and then pour liquid over the fruit bag in the fermenter. Add water to bring the volume up to 5 gallons. Allow to cool overnight.

3. Pitch yeast and allow to ferment for at least three weeks or when primary fermentation has ceased. Remove fruit bag and gently squeeze juice.

4. Rack wine into carboy and attach fermentation lock.

5. For dry mead, allow the mead to sit in a dark, cool place for four to six months. Rack every three weeks until mead is clear. Bottle when wine is ready.

6. If you wish to add carbonation, you can add ¼ tsp white table sugar per 12 oz bottle, or stir in ½ lb to 1 lb raw honey. Dissolve the honey in boiling water first and cool. Rack every three weeks until mead is clear.

7. Allow mead to age for six months to a year.

Cherry the Mead You're With

Yield 1 Gallon/3.8 L

OG = 1.090 FG = 1.014 ABV = 10%

Ingredients

- Pomace (cherry fruit solid) from "Cherry the Wine You're With" in Chapter 4
- Water
- 13 lbs (2.7 kg) honey
- Mead Yeast
- 1 tsp tannin
- 1-gallon carboy

Instructions

1. Place the pomace in a sterilized fermenter.

2. Heat 1 gallon of water to a boil and after you remove the pot from the heat, stir in the honey to dissolve. Allow the mixture to cool.

3. Bring the level up to 5 gallons and dissolve the tannin. Measure out another gallon of water.

4. Pitch the yeast. Allow to ferment. Check daily to see if the fruit is on top. If it is, punch it down with a sterilized spoon or paddle.

5. After a week strain out the fruit. Add more water to bring back up to the 5-gallon mark.

6. Allow mead to sit for two months.

7. For dry mead, allow the mead to sit in a dark, cool place for four to six months. Rack every three weeks until mead is clear. Bottle when wine is ready.

8. If you wish to add carbonation, you can add ¼ tsp white table sugar per 12 oz bottle, or stir in ½ lb to 1 lb raw honey. Dissolve the honey in boiling water first and cool. Rack every three weeks until mead is clear.

9. Allow mead to age for six months to a year.

Methleglin

The Vikings' favorite drink was mead. They believed it was sent from the gods. The Vikings believed when they died in battle they would ascend to Valhalla, which was a giant mead hall for fallen warriors.

Here is a story about mead and the Norse God Odin. There was a wise creature called Kvasir whose knowledge and wisdom were so legendary that the two dwarves, Fiallar and Gallar became jealous. In their fit of jealous rage they killed Kvasir in order to draw his wisdom from him. They mixed honey with his blood and brewed it into mead, which became known as the "Holy Mead" or "Mead of Inspiration." It was believed that if anyone drank the mead he or she would gain wisdom. If the person was already wise, drinking the mead would give them god-like wisdom.

A giant called Gilling caught the dwarves for the murder of the Kvasir. The giant's son required the dwarves to deposit their mead into three vessels, which were known as Odhroerir (Inspiration), Son (Offering), and Boden (Expiation). Two guardians, Suttung and his daughter Gunlod, watched over the mead that was secured in a mountain.

Odin's two ravens, named Huginn (Thought) and Muninn (Memory), reported to Odin what had occurred. Odin set off to gather the Holy Mead. In barter for Odin's work, he went to Baugi, who was Suttung's brother, to ask to be let into Gunlod's chamber. Baugi did not want to do this but he faced losing his harvest so he bore a hole through the rock, which led into Gunlod's chamber. Once inside Odin was able to seduce Gunlod and during the process took a sip some of the Holy Mead. Rather than swallowing, he held the mead in his mouth. He drained the contents of all three containers.

Odin escaped with the mead and discharged it into three containers in his home of Asgaard. The mead was hidden in a well, or in some versions, a cup next to the well. The three vessels were named Heiddraupnir (light dropper); Hoddrofnir (treasure opener); and Odhroerir (exciter of the heart). The three vessels belong to the three Norns or Wyrd sisters.

Erik the Viking Mead

This is a versatile recipe in that you can use different amounts of honey to create different results. The more honey you add, the sweeter the mead. This also depends on the type of yeast you use as higher alcohol-tolerant yeasts will produce a drier, more alcoholic mead.

Yield 5 Gallons/19 L

OG = 1.088 FG = 1.014 ABV = 10%

Ingredients:

- 8 to 10 lbs pure, raw honey (produces a light mead) *or* 12 to 13 lbs pure, raw honey (produces medium sweet mead) *or* 15 to 16 lbs pure, raw honey (produces a very sweet or higher alcohol mead)

- Water

- 3 tsp yeast nutrient

- 1 tsp acid blend

- 5 to 7 oz freshly sliced ginger root

- ¼ tsp fresh rosemary (you should use less if using dried rosemary.)

- 5 to 6 whole cloves (be careful, as this can overwhelm the taste of your mead)

- 1 to 2 vanilla beans (this is optional; do not use vanilla extract)

- 1 tsp cinnamon and/or nutmeg (This is optional. Be creative, but always remember that less is more. You can always add more but you cannot take away as desired.)

- 2 to 3 lemon, lime, and/or orange peels (You should add to your preference. If you add more than 2 to 3 you may consider reducing your acid blend.)

- 2 to 3 cups crushed fruit (You can use fresh peaches, strawberries, plums, or grapes. You can use frozen but you may want to defrost it first and reduce your water slightly.)

- 1 packet yeast (mead yeast comes in different types such as dry or sweet. If you cannot locate mead yeast you can use champagne or ale yeast. The champagne yeast can produce sparkling mead.)

- Nylon bag/cheesecloth

- Standard winemaking equipment

Instructions:

1. Boil the water for 10 to 15 minutes.

2. Remove the water from the heat and stir in and slowly dissolve the honey.

3. Add the yeast nutrients, acid blend, and spices (rosemary, ginger, vanilla, cinnamon, nutmeg, cloves, fruit peels). Make sure all the honey is dissolved, and boil the mixture for another 10 to 15 minutes. Do not over-boil or you will destroy some of the natural honey flavor. You will notice some foam forming on top of the mixture; this is normal. Skim it off as needed.

4. Turn off heat, and add crushed fruit (You can place the fruit in cheesecloth if you prefer). Allow the fruit to steep 15 to 30 minutes.

5. Remove the fruit, and if needed use a hand skimmer. Pour the mead through strainer or cheesecloth into 5-gallon fermentation vessel.

6. Allow the mead to cool for about 24 hours.

7. Extract a cup of the mead and heat it. Do not allow it to boil. Stir in your mead yeast. Let it sit for five to 15 minutes. Add this mead/yeast mixture to fermentation vessel and swirl it around. If you are using liquid mead yeast, you can add it directly to the mead. Add water to increase liquid to 5-gallon level.

8. Place the lid on the vessel and add your fermentation lock on top. Place the mead in a dark place that is not too cool for seven days.

9. After seven days, siphon and rack off into a carboy. Attach airlock.

10. For dry mead, allow the mead to sit in a dark, cool place for four to six months. Rack every three weeks until mead is clear. Bottle when wine is ready.

11. If you wish to add carbonation, you can add ¼ tsp of white table sugar per 12 oz bottle, or stir in ½ lb to 1 lb raw of honey. You will want to dissolve the honey in boiling water first and cool it. Rack every three weeks until mead is clear.

Simple Methleglin

Yield: 5 gallons/19 L

OG = 0.997 FG = 1.024 ABV = 9%

Ingredients:

- 12 lbs Desert Honey (or some other lighter honey)
- ½ oz fresh ginger root, peeled and finely chopped
- 1 whole nutmeg, grated
- ½ tsp whole cloves
- 5 cinnamon sticks, each 2 inches long, broken up
- Water
- 5 tsp yeast nutrient
- 2 tsp acid blend
- Yeast
- 1 campden tablet
- Mead yeast
- Standard winemaking equipment

Instructions:

1. Bring water to a boil. Add all the ingredients except yeast and bring up to 165 degrees F/74 degrees C for 45 min.

2. Cool the must and strain out the spices. When it has reached room temperature pitch yeast. Let sit for one month.

3. Rack into carboy and add a campden tablet.

4. For sweeter mead add 2 lbs of honey and allow it to sit for another two months. Bottle.

5. For a drier mead, rack every three weeks until mead is clear. Bottle when the wine is ready.

Lemon Ginger Snap Methleglin

Yield: 5 gallons/19 L

OG = 1.086 FG = 1.026 ABV = 6%

Ingredients:

- 7.1 lbs honey
- 5 lbs sugar
- 3 tbsp sliced ginger
- 1 tsp ground mace
- 1+ tsp fresh rosemary
- 8 large lemons
- 4 slices of whole-wheat bread
- Mead yeast
- Nylon bag/cheesecloth

Instructions:

1. Dissolve sugar and honey in gently boiling water. Skim off the foam that forms on top. As it begins to boil add ginger, mace, rosemary, bread, and the grated peel of the lemons.

2. Remove the pith from the lemons and discard. Cut the lemons in half, and squeeze them into the must. Place remaining fruit in a bag/cheesecloth. Place bag in the must.

3. Boil mixture at 180 degrees F for 20 to 30 minutes. Quickly cool mixture and pour into fermentation vessel. Bring liquid up to 5-gallon level. Pitch yeast.

4. Let sit for one month.

5. Strain and rack into carboy and add a campden tablet.

6. For sweeter mead, add 2 lbs of honey and allow it to sit for another two months. Bottle.

7. For a drier mead, rack every three weeks until mead is clear. Bottle when the wine is ready.

Lovely Lavender Mead

Yield 1 Gallon/3.8 L

OG = 1.04 FG = 1.014 ABV = 10%

Ingredients:

- 4 lbs honey
- 1 pint lavender flowers (fresh, not dried)
- ½ tsp tannin powder
- ¼ tsp citric acid
- 1 tsp yeast nutrient
- ½ tsp champagne yeast
- 1-gallon carboy

Instructions:

1. Boil honey and ½ gallon water for five minutes. Skim foam off the top.

2. Add flowers, citric acid, and tannin in a gallon jug and pour the hot liquid over them.

3. Allow the mixture to cool. Pitch yeast and add yeast nutrient. Attach the airlock.

4. Let ferment one week, and then strain out flowers. Rack and allow to sit for two months.

5. Check SG and when it is stable, bottle.

6. Allow to mature for six months to a year.

Autumn Olive Mead

Yield: 5 gallons/19 L

OG = 1.100 FG = 1.000 ABV = 13.5%

Ingredients:

- 6 to 8 lbs freshly picked autumn olives
- 6 to 8 lbs brown sugar (Jaggery, Indian palm sugar, works fantastic)
- 1 quart unsweetened cherry juice
- 8 to 10 lbs honey
- Red wine yeast
- Tannin
- 5 tsp yeast nutrient
- 2 tsp acid blend or malic acid (aim for pH 3.5 or so)
- 1 campden tablet
- 1 lb of beets for color
- Standard winemaking equipment
- Pectic enzyme- follow instructions on bottle

Instructions:

1. Steep autumn olives in a quart of boiled water. Strain and discard berries. Steep beets in a quart of boiled water. Strain the beets and retain juice. Mix beet water and olive water.

2. Boil brown sugar and honey in water. Skim from foam that will form on the top.

3. Cool mixture and add campden tablet. Allow it to sit overnight.

4. Test specific gravity. It should be about 1.085; may want to sweeten up to 1100. Add malic acid or acid blend to get pH back down to 3.5.

5. Add water to bring up to 5-gallon level. Pitch red wine yeast.

6. Ferment to dry or near dry (FG 0.990 to 1). Add campden tablet. Sweeten to taste to about 1.010, which is about 2 1/2 cups of sugar per 5 gallons.

7. Bottle and let sit for a few months. Initially it will be a bit too strong in terms of an earthy odor but this will mellow with time.

Sweet Meads

These are the simple forms of meads such as sack mead, which is a sweeter type. These have extra sugars or a much more honey added. These have a sweeter flavor, but they also have a higher potential alcohol content.

Maple Leaf Mead

Yield: 5 gallons/19 L

OG = 1.100 FG = 1.000 ABV = 13.5%

Ingredients:

- 5 lbs light clover honey
- 2 lbs dark wildflower honey
- 6 lbs maple syrup
- Water to make 5 gallons
- 2 tbsp yeast nutrient
- Sweet mead yeast
- Standard winemaking equipment

Instructions:

1. Boil about 4 gallons of water. Remove from heat and add honey and maple syrup. Stir well to dissolve. Reduce the temperature of mixture clearly either by ice bath or wort chiller. Reduce temperature quickly and place in primary fermenter. Add water to bring to 5-gallon level. Pitch yeast.

2. Allow to ferment for two weeks.

3. Rack to carboy. Allow to sit for two months. Bottle.

4. The longer you allow it to mature the smoother the taste.

New World Order Sack Mead

Yield: 5 gallons/19 L

OG = 1.100 FG = 1.000 ABV = 10%

Ingredients:

- 11 ¾ lbs wildflower honey
- 5 lbs fresh strawberries
- 2 lbs fresh kiwi
- 2 pomegranates (seed and fruit)
- 1 tsp yeast nutrient
- Sweet mead yeast
- Water
- Cheesecloth/nylon bag
- Standard winemaking equipment

Instructions:

1. Cut and destem the fruit. Place fruit in the cheesecloth/bag. Boil the bag in 3 quarts of water for 20 minutes. Add the honey and skim off any foam that forms for another 20 minutes. Place mixture and fruit bag in the primary fermentation vessel. Cool overnight.

2. Bring liquid up to 5-gallon level with water. Add nutrient and pitch yeast.

3. In 10 days rack to carboy. Discard fruit bag. Wait until primary fermentation has completely stopped.

4. Rack mead again to clear.

5. Allow mead to settle for three months, then rack. Bottle mead when the hydrometer readings are stable.

6. Allow mead to age for about two years.

CASE STUDY: CHRIS MINNICK

www.badastronauts.com
chris@minnick.com
You can buy my grapefruit wine at Revolution Wines, 2116 P Street, Sacramento, CA 95811:
www.revolution-wines.com
Home winemaker

I have been making wine at home for four years. First of all, I love the end product. But I also began to understand wine on a completely different level than just appreciation of it as a beverage. The study of wine and winemaking touches on so many different subjects — biology, chemistry, history, agriculture, art, music, engineering, marketing, and more — that it's impossible to ever get bored with it.

When I moved to California from Michigan, I became obsessed with wine. Just drinking it and knowing that I liked it wasn't enough. I needed to know how to make it. It also helped that I was broke, so the thought of making my own wine seemed like a good solution to my growing appetite for fermented grape juice. I made my first batch of wine from a 6-gallon kit. Shortly thereafter, I discovered that a neighbor of ours made wine on a larger scale (several 60-gallon barrels a year). I helped him for a couple years, and then started making my own barrels of wine with several friends.

When fresh grapes aren't available, I get impatient and make beer or experiment with wines made from various seasonal fruits (apples, grapefruit, and lemon so far). I have a 2007 Cabernet Sauvignon/Cabernet Franc blend. The Cab started its life as a very troubled wine. With a lot of research and attention, I was able to massage it into a very good wine, which ended up winning several awards. My 2008 Galactic Grapefruit Wine, which can be found in this book, was my second batch of grapefruit wine made from grapefruit grown on my backyard tree. I made 30 gallons of it.

CASE STUDY: CHRIS MINNICK

My advice to new home winemakers is to read everything you can about winemaking. There's a lot of information out there, but much of it is conflicting. Winemaking is an art, a science, and a craft. You're likely to find someone who will tell you just about anything is the "right way." In the end, it's up to you to do your homework, gain your own experience, and trust your instincts.

If you keep a clean home winery, you shouldn't have to add a lot of sulfites. I don't believe that adding sulfites is a bad thing necessarily; even what some would consider to be a lot.

Any amount that can't be detected in the taste or smell is ok. The real problem is if you're adding a lot of sulfites because your sanitation practices are lacking.

My grape wines have received numerous awards, including a double gold and best red of show from the El Dorado County Fair, and a Gold from the California State Fair. I recommend other winemakers enter competitions. It's a good chance to get some feedback on all your hard work from people who have tasted a lot of wine.

For someone new to home winemaking I would recommend they buy the following supplies:

- Food-grade bucket for fermenting
- 6-gallon carboy
- Stopper
- Airlock
- Racking tube
- A decent corker
- Hydrometer
- pH meter

After a time, if you really serious about winemaking beyond just a simple hobby, I would suggest you purchase the following:

- Acid test kit
- Refractometer
- A large (#40) press
- A crusher/destemmer with a motor
- Large truck

My food pairing with wild wine is pizza, because it goes with everything.

CHAPTER 8

Wild Wine Drinks

The wild wines you create in this book are fantastic. Even great wines can become legendary drinks with just a little help and mixology. This chapter contains recipes of combining your wild wines to create wild beverages.

How About a Punch

Ingredients:

- 2 fifths champagne
- 2 fifths fruit wine, red
- 2 fifths fruit wine, white
- 2 oz lime juice
- 3 tsp of grated lime peel
- 1 quart frozen strawberries

Instructions:

1. Simmer frozen strawberries, lime peel, and lime juice in a pan for ten minutes over low heat.

2. Pour the liquid in a punch bowl with a block of ice and wine and champagne.

Fires at Night Punch

Ingredients:

- 1 bottle Stone Fruit wine
- 1 handful Sweet Woodruff Herb
- 2 cups fresh, sliced strawberries
- 2 tsp sugar

Instructions

1. Add wine, sugar, and herbs to a punch bowl and stir lightly. Cover the mixture, and allow it to sit overnight in the refrigerator.

2. Strain out the woodruff. Add strawberry slices and serve cold.

Arrgh!

Ingredients

- 2 oz spiced rum
- 2 oz fruit wine
- Cola
- 1 slice lime

Instructions:

1. Combine rum and wine in a glass. Add ice and top off with cola. Garnish with the lime slice.

Cranky Peach

Ingredients:

- ¼ oz Schnapps, peach
- 3 oz white wine
- Carbonated water/club soda
- 2 oz cranberry juice
- ¼ oz sour mix
- ¼ oz simple sugar syrup

Instructions:

1. Pour the ingredients in a highball glass with ice. Add the club soda last after stirring the rest.

Blue Skies

Ingredients:

- 1 splash Curacao, blue
- 5 oz dry mead
- 1 oz carbonated water/club Soda
- 1 twist of peel lemon

Instructions:

1. Pour wine in a glass with ice. Top off drink with carbonated soda and Curacao. Add the lemon as a garnish.

Bitter Cherries

Ingredients:

- ½ tsp liqueur, maraschino
- 1 ½ oz cherry wine
- 1 dash bitters, orange
- 1 tbsp pineapple juice

Instructions:

1. Combine ingredients in a cocktail shaker with ice. Shake and strain into a cocktail glass.

Compare Campari

Ingredients:

- 3 ⅓ oz Campari
- 1 bottle peach wine
- 1 bottle carbonated water/club soda
- 3 whole lemon
- 1 whole, small orange

Instructions:

1. Squeeze the juice from the lemons into a punch bowl. Add some ice, wine soda, and top with Campari. Mix in slices of orange and lemon.

Cider Shots Sangria

Ingredients:

- 4 shots gin
- 2 shots Sour Apple Pucker
- 2 shots Sour Watermelon Pucker
- 3 shots vodka
- 1 bottle watermelon wine
- 1 whole orange
- 2 glasses cider
- ¼ cup lime juice
- 2 cups orange juice
- 2 whole apples
- 1 whole lime
- 1 package strawberries

Instructions:

1. Cut the apples into cubes and slice the oranges, limes, and strawberries and place into a punch bowl. Pour the cider and wine into a pitcher or a punch bowl. Add to this the juices, gin, puckers, and finally the vodka. Stir the concoction well. To add a little fun you can add pomegranate sugar to the rim of your glass. Use a ladle to pour drinks into the cups carefully so you do not remove the sugar on the rims.

Tropical Delight

Ingredients:

- 3 oz white wine
- 2 oz carbonated water/club soda
- 1 oz pineapple juice
- Lemonade
- 1 tsp sugar, powdered
- 1 shot Schnapps, peach
- 1 shot vodka
- Pineapple wine

Instructions:

1. Pour the wine, vodka, peach Schnapps, sugar, pineapple juice, soda, and lemonade to taste into a shaker with ice. Shake and serve.

Sunrise Sangria

Ingredients:

- 2 oz orange wine
- 1 oz grapefruit wine
- 4 oz lemon-lime soda
- 1 tbsp lemon juice
- 1 oz orange juice
- 1 slice of lemon
- 1 slice of orange
- 1 tbsp sugar

Instructions:

1. Pour lemon juice and sugar into a wine glass. Stir the sugar well until it completely dissolves. Add ice to the glass and add the orange wine, grapefruit wine, and orange juice. Stir and add the lemon-lime soda. Finish by garnishing with lemon and orange slices.

Cherry Baby

Ingredients:

- 1 part vodka
- 1 part tequila
- 2 parts cherry wine
- 1 splash lemon-lime soda
- 1 splash water
- 1 tsp sugar

Instructions:

1. Add the ingredients except the lemon-lime soda to a shaker. Shake well. Strain over ice in a glass. Top off with lemon-lime soda. Add a cherry as a garnish.

Honey Trail

Ingredients:

- 3 tsp liqueur, maraschino
- 1 ½ oz sweet mead
- ¼ oz pineapple juice

Instructions:

1. Add the ingredients to a cocktail shaker and shake well. Strain over ice.

April Rain

Ingredients:

- 2 shots brandy
- 5 oz apricot wine
- 1 whole peach

Instructions

1. Cut up the peach and remove the pit. Add the peach to a blender and puree. As you do this, add the shots of brandy. When it has liquefied, add to glass. Add chilled wine and stir to mix the peach mixture and the wine.

Simple Wine Spritzer

One of my first experiences with wine was with my mother. She used to love wine spritzers and I have been a fan of them because of her.

Ingredients:

- 3 oz any white fruit wine
- 1 oz carbonated water/club soda

Instructions:

1. Combine ingredients in a white wine glass.

Ten Common Winemaking Problems

There are a number of factors that can go wrong with making a wine. That is part of the excitement in that you are able to overcome these challenges and create world-class wild wines. In this chapter I have included the ten most common errors. I have made hundreds of wines and I am still referring to this list. If you remember nothing else, remember that having sanitized hands and equipment with solve more than 90 percent of the problems that can negatively affect your wine.

> "Focus on the process and always have fun. Don't worry about whether it will be award-winning wine; what matters is that you enjoy what you produce."
> *Joe Henderkott*

CHAPTER 9

No. 1 — Wine is too acidic.

You notice that the wine has a real tart taste after you have fermented it. The solution is to cold stabilize it. This means that you will have to store your wine in a place that is close to freezing. You do not want to freeze your wine; you just want to make it very cold. The acid molecules will crystallize and fall to the bottom of the fermenter. You will need to rack the wine off these acid crystals. Taste your wine after racking. You may need to repeat the process again.

No. 2 — My wine has bubbles.

Carbonation can be caused by refermentation or it could be that your wine has been infected. You can stir the wine and de-gas it. If it has been infected, try to add some sulfites. You may have to pour out the wine if the flavor, color, or aroma changes.

No. 3 — My wine is "blah."

This can be caused by the lack of acid or tannin in your wine. This gives wine a bland taste. You can add a teaspoon of lemon juice or some strong black tea.

No. 4 — I cannot see through my wine: cloudy or hazy wine.

Your wine can become hazy due to protein matter, pectin, starch, or metallic contamination. Most of the time, yeasts will remove protein haze during fermentation. There are times racking alone will not remove cloudiness from your wine.

A simple way to clear your wine is to add a little egg white, or you can bake some eggs shells until they become dry. Crush the eggshells into the wine and allow the proteins to be drawn to the bottom. You can then rack your wine again.

You can buy a number of different clearing agents mentioned earlier in this book. You can try different ones to see if it improves your wine.

Because you are creating wild wines, many of them contain pectin that can make a wine hazy. That is why many of them have the inclusion of a pectic enzyme that will break down pectin and prevent haziness from occurring. If you did not add pectic enzyme in the beginning of the process and you believe that you have a pectin haze, you can add a tablespoon to your wine and place it in a cool place for a few days. This should clear things up.

Bacteria can cause some haziness. If you notice a bad odor or taste, it may be time to dump your wine. Make sure you sterilize your equipment thoroughly before starting again. If you see a wine mother form on your wine, you may need to buy a new fermenter, as this may hide and spoil future batches of your wine.

No. 5 — My wine is too sweet.

Sometimes your wine can have what is called a stuck fermentation. For whatever reason the yeast you added are not doing their job. The conditions may not be right or the yeast may have died off. Sometimes this can happen if you racked your wine too soon.

You can solve this problem by raising the temperature slightly to see if the yeast comes back to life. Another solution is to start over and add a new packet of yeast. Sometimes the yeast just needs an extra boost. You can do this by teaspoonful of lemon juice or yeast nutrient.

No. 6 — My yeast seems tired.

Sometimes fermentation can be slowed by weak yeast or yeast that needs a boost. You can fix this problem by adding a yeast energizer. You can also raise the temperature slightly. If it stops altogether too soon, you may need to add some more yeast.

No. 7 — My wine smells like rotten eggs.

This is caused by hydrogen sulfide, and usually occurs at the end of fermentation. There could be a number reasons for this such as contamination, too many sulfites, or not enough nutrients for the yeast. The earlier you catch the problem the more likely it will be that you can fix it before you have to dump it.

Some people will recommend copper sulfate, but this is poisonous. Instead, rack your wine and splash it as you go. Oxygen will help counteract the effects of hydrogen sulfide. You can pour the wine over some copper wire to counteract it as well. Fining agents and filtration can also remove some of the smell. I recommend some egg white or gelatin fining agents.

No. 8 — My wine smells like dirt.

Wine that smells like mushrooms or earth are the victim of tainted cork or Trichloronisole (TCA). There is no cure for this. Dump your wine. In the future you might want to consider synthetic corks or make sure that you bathe your corks in a sanitizing solution before you use them.

No. 9 — My white wine is now turning red.

This can be caused by oxidization. It has been exposed to too much oxygen. The taste will be flat. Pour it out.

No. 10 — My white wine tastes like vinegar.

The reason that wine can have a vinegar or sherry flavor can be from oxidation. It can also be because the wine has been contaminated and has become vinegar. Dump the wine and get rid of the bucket. Make sure you sanitize all your equipment very well before using it again.

CASE STUDY: TIMOTHY SKOK

Home winemaker

I used to be a beer brewer in Longmont, Colorado, during college. Then I moved out to California to get into the wine business. My roommate Jonathan Tyer was a photographer from Boston who moved to California for the same reason. Both of us are passionate about wine. We each made wine in our teens with our parents on the East coast. We used recipes using grape concentrate or frozen grapes from California. Together we combined our efforts, and to save money we do everything ourselves, and have a lot of fun with our friends and family making the wine.

Living in wine country, there are many hobby home winemakers. Most go to a store, buy their equipment, and buy their grapes or juice from someone on the Internet. For us, our recipe is all about connections. We borrow equipment from friends who work at wineries. We do improvise a lot; our winery is an insulated plywood room in our garage, with a window air conditioning unit and a baby humidifier. We sealed the cracks with duct tape and spray foam to keep it as cool as possible. We use sanitized plastic bins to pick grapes and sometimes to ferment and crush fruit in. We use the garden hose for cleaning and the bathtub to sanitize the equipment in.

For the grapes and our wine, we save money by going to vineyards and employing the help of our friends and family to pick and prune the vines. We repay them by having a barbecue in the vineyard after a long day's work.

We don't make a lot of wine (three barrels in 2008), but there are a lot of people who have fun with us. The lovely ladies next door helped us stomp the syrah grapes to get some of the backbone of the tannins from the stems. Currently we have a barrel of Syrah aging in French oak. We also have a barrel of a Cabernet Sauvignon/Merlot blend that was picked by us, my parents, and my aunt and uncles.

We are looking to experiment with some chardonnay and some Grenache and Mourvedre to make a Rhone-style blend.

2008 vintage:

Squeaky Tyer Pinot Noir Rose (inspired by the squeaking of the wheel on the garage door every time we open it)

Rhone Racer Syrah (with a photo of my 1966 mustang on it, because it evicted the mustang from the garage)

Jojoti "Joe-Joti" Bordeaux blend (Jonathan and Tim, we were trying to think of a sleek name that would incorporate our names)

Last Call

> "By making this wine vine known to the public, I have rendered my country as great a service as if I had enabled it to pay back the national debt."
>
> *Thomas Jefferson*

Wine permeates every part of our lives, history, culture, and even the arts. It is one thing to taste a great wine with a memorable dinner somewhere in Napa, Valley California. It is something else to be able to create a great wine and sipping it with a simple dinner in Davenport, Iowa.

Wine is simple to make and wild wine is no exception. This book contains many recipes to try but it is my hope that it inspires the reader to create some of their own memorable wines and memorable times.

Appendix A

Wine Yeast Strains

There are a lot of different types of yeast strains you can purchase. The thing to keep in mind is that the name of the yeast strain refers to the type of grape from which they were harvested. The yeast strains that are created in laboratories usually have a number associated with them. The column with the heading "Alcohol tolerance" refers to the highest percentage of alcohol in the wine that the yeast can withstand before they begin to die off.

Dry Yeast Packets

Name	Brand	Type of Wine	Alcohol Tolerance
Narbonne 71B-1122	Lavlin	White/Blush	14%
ChampagneEC-1118	Lavlin	Cider. Late harvest, stuck fermentations, sparkling	18%
Montpellier K1V-1116	Lavlin	Fruit wines	18%
Red Wine RC-212	Lavlin	Red, Berry	12%-14%
White Wine ICV-D-47	Lavlin	White, Rose, Mead	15%
Montrachet	Red Star	All Purpose, Vegetable, Grain	13%
Premier Cuvee	Red Star	White, melons	18%
Pasteur Champagne	Red Star	Sparkling, Mead	15%
Cote des Blancs	Red Star	Orchard Fruits, White	14%
Red Pasteur	Red Star	Red, Berries	16%
Saccharomyces Cerevisiae AW4	Vintner's Harvest	Dry White Wines	14.50%
Saccharomyces Cerevisiae BV7	Vintner's Harvest	Sweeter White Wine	13%
Saccharomyces Bayanus CL23	Vintner's Harvest	Blush, Dry, Citrus	18%

Saccharomyces Cerevisiae CR51	Vintner's Harvest	Red, Berries	13.50%
Saccharomyces Cerevisiae CY17	Vintner's Harvest	Fruit Wines, Blush	15%
Saccharomyces Cerevisiae MA33	Vintner's Harvest	Fruit Wines, Blush, herbal, grain	14%
Saccharomyces Cerevisiae R56	Vintner's Harvest	Zinfandel, Light tasting fruit wines	13.50%
Saccharomyces Cerevisiae SN9	Vintner's Harvest	Aged wines, pit wines, berries	18%
Saccharomyces Cerevisiae VR21	Vintner's Harvest	Red, Berries, Fruit	15%

Liquid Yeast

Name	Brand	Type of Wine	Alcohol Tolerance
Champagne	White Labs	Sparkling, Strawberry, Raspberry	17%
Avise Wine Yeast	White Labs	Mixed White, Pear, Peach, Grapefruit	15%
Sweet Mead and Wine	White Labs	Dandelion, Mead, Fruit, Plum	15%
Steinberg-Geisenheim Wine Yeast	White Labs	Dandelion, Light Fruit, Root	14%
Chardonnay White Wine	White Labs	White, Light Fruit, Herb	14%
French White Wine Yeast	White Labs	White, Mead, Rice, Grain	16%
Merlot Red Wine Yeast	White Labs	Red, Berry, Heavy Red Fruit	18%
Assmanshausen Wine Yeast	White Labs	Blush, Mixed, Strawberry, Berry	16%
French Red Wine Yeast	White Labs	Red, Berry, Heavy Red, Fruit	17%

Cabernet Red Wine Yeast	White Labs	Heavy Red, Chocolate, Vegetable	16%
Suremain Burgundy Wine Yeast	White Labs	Pit, Red	16%
English Cider	White Labs	Apples, Pit, Mead, Grain	14.00%
Pasteur Champagne	Wyeast	Sparkling, Champagne, Strawberry, Raspberry	17%
Chateau Red	Wyeast	Cherry, Berry, Red	14%
Sake #9	Wyeast	Mead, Rice, Grain, Plum, Sake	16.00%
Sweet Mead	Wyeast	Mead, Pit, Seeded	11%
Chablis	Wyeast	Fruity Whites	12%
Chianti	Wyeast	Cherry, Berry, Red	14.00%
Bordeaux	Wyeast	Red, Heavy Fruit	14%
Eau de Vie	Wyeast	Barleywine, High Alcohol Red	21%
Dry Mead	Wyeast	Herb, Cyser, Mead, Fruit Mead	18%

Cider	Wyeast	Apple, Peach, Cherry, Mead	12%
Port wine	Wyeast	Heavy Red, Cherry, Raspberry, Blueberry	14%
Rudesheimer	Wyeast	Ice Wines, Meads, Sweet Cider	12%
Zinfandel	Wyeast	High Sugar Fruit	18%

Tales from the Vineyard

Tale No. 1

A friend of mine once had a little mishap when she tried to make a blueberry wheat beer. After finishing primary fermentation she moved her beer to a small secondary fermentation vessel and added store-bought blueberries. Because of the added sugar, the blueberries began to ferment. I was at her place watching the foam come out of the airlock and asked her if she was going to replace the airlock with a blow off tube. She said it would be fine. The next morning I received two pictures in my e-mail of the resulting explosion. A single blueberry became lodged in the airlock causing the pressure to build. The beer shot about 9 feet into the air and left about 3 gallons of liquid on the floor. A year later she sold her house and we were still finding blueberry particles on the walls and ceiling.

Joe Henderkott, home winemaker

Tale No. 2

Once I learned a powerful lesson about friendship and winemaking. I was cleaning the hose that was used to transfer wine from one vessel to another while it was still connected to an electric pump. I was holding the extension cord. My "friend" was holding the hoses. The output end of the hose should have been pointed anywhere but at me when I plugged in the pump. It wasn't, and I got quite a shock I got a wine sticky wine shower. It's funny now, but not so funny at the time. *Chris Minnick, home winemaker*

Tale No. 3

I bottled blackberry wine one year and gave my daughter a bottle. She put it in a wine rack on top of a table in her bedroom. It was winter and her house was pretty warm from the furnace. One day she came home from work and the bottle had exploded across the room due to a secondary fermentation in the bottle. Her white comforter on the bed had caught 98 percent of it. She called me in disgust but was able to wash it out without staining and we laugh about it now. *Lynn Keay, home winemaker*

Glossary of Terms

Aging- Allowing wine to sit in a cool place for six months to a year to improve the taste. This is sometimes done in oak barrels.

Airlock/Fermentation Lock- This is a device that allows carbon dioxide to be released from a vessel without allowing oxygen to get into the wine.

Autolysis- This is the process of yeast breaking down the sediment in a fermentation vessel. It can lead to off flavors in a wine.

Camden Tablet- This is a tablet that contains potassium metabisulfate. It is used to sterilize wine.

Cap- This is formed when fruit floats to the top of a must and is then punched down during early fermentation.

Bentonite- A clay used for clearing, or fining a wine.

Balling/Brix- This is a measure on a hydrometer that calculates the specific gravity or sugar content of a liquid.

Carboy- This is a glass jug that comes in different sizes and is usually used during secondary fermentation.

Dry- This a term to describe when all the sugars have been fermented. It is the opposite of sweet.

Hydrometer- This is an instrument that measures the specific gravity or density of a wine.

Isinglass- This is a type of fining agent that is made from the parts of a sturgeon.

Lees-These are dead yeasts that form a type of sludge at the bottom of a fermenter. Usually, the wine is racked off these lees because leaving them can impart negative flavors in a finished wine.

Must- This is the term for fermenting juice before it becomes a wine.

Oxidation-This is what occurs when wine is exposed to oxygen. It can destroy a wine.

pH- The level of acidity in wine. It can be tested with an acid testing kit, and be adjusted by adding different acids such as citric acid or acids blends. If the wine is too acidic, a base must be added or the must is diluted.

Pitch Yeast- This is the act of adding yeast to a wine must.

Racking- This is the act of siphoning clear wine off lees in a carboy. This process helps clear a wine by leaving particulars behind. It sometimes takes a few different rackings to get a wine totally clear.

Still Wine- Wine that has no bubbles.

Sparkling- Wine that has bubbles, like champagne.

Stuck wine- This is when fermentation has stopped.

Sweet Wine- This is opposite of dry wine and contains at least 3 percent sugar after it has fermented.

Tannin- This is contained in the skins of grapes and gives wine astringency.

Vintage- This is the year a wine was created.

Bibliography

www.museum.upenn.edu/new/exhibits/online_exhibits/wine/winein-tro.html

http://scorpius.spaceports.com/~goodwine/vegwinerec.htm

http://scorpius.spaceports.com/~goodwine/fruitwinerec.htm

http://blue-n-gold.com/halfdan/meadrecp.htm

www.washingtonwinemaker.com

www.talisman.com/mead

www.winepress.us

www.drinknation.com

Resources

Web sites

http://forum.northernbrewer.com

http://morewinemaking.com

www.winemaking.jackkeller.net

www.Winebusiness.com

www.napafermentation.com

www.eckraus.com

www.breworganic.com

www.midwestsupplies.com

Books

Spence, P. *Mad About Mead: The Nectar of the Gods.* St. Paul: Llewellyn Worldwide, 1997.

Proulx, A., Nicols, L. *Cider Making, Using and Enjoying Sweet and Hard Cider.* Maine: Storey Publishing, 2003.

Marie, D. *Wild Wines: Creating Organic Wines from Nature's Garden.* NY: Square One. 2008.

Spaziani, G. *The Home Winemaker's Companion: Secrets, Recipes, and Know-how for Making 115 Great Tasting Wines.* Maine: Storey Publishing, 2000.

Cox, J. *From Vines to Wines: The Complete Guide to Growing Grapes and Making Your Own Wine.* Maine: Storey Books. 1999.

Vargas, P., Gulling, R. *Making Wild Wines and Meads: 125 Unusual Recipes Using Herbs, Fruits, Flowers and More.* Maine: Storey Publishing. 1999.

Author Biography

John is an award-winning amateur winemaker who lives with his wife and two daughters in Winston-Salem, North Carolina. When John is not writing and making wine, he plays the piccolo in the Western Piedmont Symphony.

Index

S

Sack Mead, 210, 250-251

Sour, 22, 98, 122, 124, 232, 237, 256, 258

Sparkling, 270, 272-273, 42, 63, 146, 209, 244, 11

Stabilizers, 58, 80

Strawberry, 272-273, 114, 222, 228, 256

Sweet Mead, 272-273, 126, 211-213, 219, 234, 244, 250-251, 260

Sweet Wine, 53, 70, 76, 121-123, 145, 155, 158, 160-161, 163-165, 169-170

T

Tannin, 75, 83, 91-94, 98-103, 105, 117-120, 123, 126, 129, 133, 135, 137-141, 145, 148, 156, 163, 192, 204, 230-231, 241-242, 248-249, 264

V

Vintage, 71, 267, 10

W

White, 270, 272-273, 276, 24-26, 29, 31, 59, 62-63, 82-83, 86-87, 112-113, 137, 140, 154-155, 173, 196, 198-199, 213-216, 219-220, 222-224, 226-229, 231-234, 236-239, 241-242, 246, 255-256, 259, 261, 264, 266, 13, 6

Y

Yeast, 269-270, 272-273, 17-20, 23, 27-31, 33, 35, 50-51, 53-54, 56-57, 59, 70-71, 74, 76-77, 79, 87, 90-115, 117-135, 137-144, 148, 152-166, 168-175, 178-180, 182-184, 187-208, 211-217, 219-252, 265-266, 10, 277-278